The Granite Landscape

A Natural History of America's Mountain Domes, from Acadia to Yosemite

The Granite Landscape

A Natural History of America's Mountain Domes, from Acadia to Yosemite

Tom Wessels

Illustrations by Brian D. Cohen

THE COUNTRYMAN PRESS, WOODSTOCK, VERMONT

First Edition

Library of Congress Cataloging-in-Publication Data
Wessels, Tom, 1951–
    The granite landscape : a natural history of America's mountain domes, from Acadia to Yosemite / Tom Wessels ; illustrations by Brian D. Cohen.
        p. cm.
    ISBN 0-88150-429-7 (alk. paper)
        1. Natural History—United States. 2. National Parks and reserves—United States. 3. Granite—United States. I. Title
    QH104 . W47 2001
    508.73—dc21   00-065977

Cover and interior design by Angie Hurlbut
Cover and interior photographs by Tom Wessels
Frontispiece photo: Looking southwest over the Tuolumne River, Yosemite National Park, by Tom Wessels
Map and diagrams on pages 5, 28, and 30 by Jacques Chazaud, © 2001 The Countryman Press

Published by The Countryman Press, P.O. Box 748, Woodstock, Vermont 05091
Distributed by W. W. Norton & Company, Inc., 500 Fifth Avenue, New York, NY 10110

Printed in the United States of America

10 9 8 7 6 5 4 3 2

To Kelsey, whose love of the natural world ranges from summit to sea

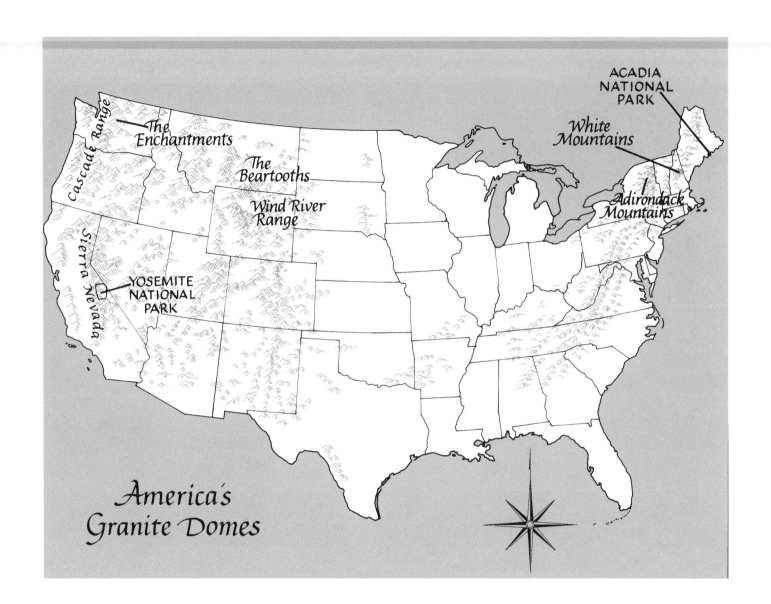

ACADIA
NATIONAL
PARK

White
Mountains

Adirondack
Mountains

Cascade Range

The
Enchantments

The Beartooths

Wind River
Range

Sierra Nevada

YOSEMITE
NATIONAL
PARK

America's
Granite Domes

Table of Contents

9   ACKNOWLEDGMENTS

11   INTRODUCTION
Black Mountain

PART ONE
THE MAKING OF GRANITE DOMES

21   CHAPTER ONE
Origins of Granite

33   CHAPTER TWO
Sculpted by Glaciers

49   CHAPTER THREE
Graced with Lichen and Moss

65   CHAPTER FOUR
Exposed by Fire and Ice

PART TWO
AMERICA'S GRANITE MOUNTAINS

77   CHAPTER FIVE
Acadia: Land of Fire and Fog

93   CHAPTER SIX
The Whites and Adirondacks: Fragile
Summits

111   CHAPTER SEVEN
The Wind Rivers: Temples of Stone

129   CHAPTER EIGHT
The Beartooths: Alpine Gardens

143   CHAPTER NINE
The Enchantments: Land of Contrasts

157   CHAPTER TEN
Yosemite: Range of Light

PART THREE
APPENDIXES

173   APPENDIX A
Geological Time Line

175   APPENDIX B
List of Plants

181   Glossary

189   Selected Bibliography

191   INDEX

Acknowledgments

This book would not have been possible without the trailblazing work of Ann Zwinger in her classic natural history, *Land Above the Trees*. Without Ann's book, I don't believe I would have developed the idea of writing a natural history of granite domes. Even the structure of this book was influenced by her work.

Thanks to all the people at The Countryman Press for bringing this book to such a handsome outcome. Marcia and Kelsey, thank you for allowing me to roam out west for two months and leave you with all the chores. Special thanks to my lifelong friend Jeff Weir for his expert advice on black-and-white photography. To my good friends Deb Frey, Eric Love, Chris Papouchis, Andrew Stemple, and Richard Thompson, my deepest gratitude, particularly to those of you who survived mosquito swarms with me. I couldn't have done my research without your good humor and companionship.

Special thanks to Susie Caldwell, who did the first edits of the manuscript and made critical suggestions on how to structure the book. Once again I am indebted to Helen Whybrow, who even after leaving The Countryman Press continued to nurture this project through her wonderful skills as editor, designer, and advocate. Finally, like our first book, *Reading the Forested Landscape,* this one would not have been possible without Brian D. Cohen's wonderful illustrations. Brian, thanks for another satisfying and fun collaboration.

Introduction:
Black Mountain

It's early afternoon during an autumn hike—perfect siesta time. Sweet meadow grass, a bed of pine needles, the base of a sand dune all provide wonderful sites, yet my best siestas have all occurred on hard, smooth, glacially polished granite. On granite there are no surface irregularities to jab at my back, no ants to run over my skin, no duff and sand to sneak down my collar; there's just clean, secure rock. Lying within a gently curved glacial groove with a rolled-up jacket for a pillow, I'm cradled like a clam in its shell.

I remember my first nap on granite. It was October 1970 on the north ridge of New Hampshire's Mount Chocorua. That fall, having just transferred from Johns Hopkins University to the University of New Hampshire, I spent every weekend hiking in the White Mountains. I had never experienced mountains as grand as these before, had never walked through a tundra landscape where heath, lichen, and sedge grew among jumbled configurations of huge, irregular, dark metamorphic boulders. Enthralled by this rugged alpine beauty, I hit summit after summit.

Then I climbed Mount Chocorua. The same climate that had cracked metamorphic bedrock into millions of bed-sized boulders on the Whites' other summits had left no mark whatsoever on Chocorua's smooth granite dome. At the time I was completely unaware why

Chocorua was so different. With no background in geology, I didn't know the difference between metamorphic schist and granite, let alone how the harsh climate following glaciation — a period characterized by dramatic freeze-thaw cycles — could reduce bedrock to a pile of boulders. Still, I could perceive that Chocorua's exposed summit was powerfully different from all the others I had experienced.

My next encounter with granite "balds" was in Acadia National Park on Mount Desert Island, Maine. Entire mountains of exposed bedrock created ledgy landscapes stretching for miles. I was hooked. I instantly knew that these marvelously open environments would become favorite haunts — places worthy of extensive exploration.

Thirty years later I have strode across enough granite ledge throughout the United States to equal half the length of the Appalachian Trail, some fifteen hundred miles. What is most striking about all these miles is their amazing similarity, whether in California, Montana, New York, or Maine. Not only is the glacially scoured granite alike from place to place, but the plant communities that colonize it strongly resemble each other, too. In fact, I know of no other American environment that shares such a uniform ecology. Like deserts, granite domes create harsh growing conditions, so only certain kinds of plants are found on them. Specific species of pine, heath, grass, moss, and lichen may change from state to state, but the ecosystems they create are so similar that someone who grew up on Mount Desert Island, Maine, would feel very much at home atop Yosemite's lofty domes. To get a sense of the kinds of features encountered on a granite dome, let's take a trip to Black Mountain.

Black Mountain — a dome of granite surrounded by a sea of metamorphic schist — stands ten miles south of my home in southern Vermont. The only granite bald in the southern half of the state, it is an anomaly, so the contrast between this mountain and the surrounding terrain is dramatic. An easy climb of less than a mile brings me to the twelve-hundred-foot summit, where I find a landscape that feels strikingly different from the forested hillsides common to the region.

The hike begins on a level woods road that winds its way through an open forest of eastern white pine. Understory plants such as red baneberry and herb Robert hint at substrates that are rich in nutrients (a common attribute of Vermont soils—they are derived from metamorphic bedrock, which holds a lot of calcium). The pines are thriving in this well-managed forest. Trees reaching one hundred feet are less than eighty years of age. When I see white pines of this stature, it reminds me that pines once reached twice this height in New England but were all cut by the British prior to the nineteenth century. Back then trees of such size wouldn't have been found on the flanks of Black Mountain—nor will they ever be. Since they might stand a hundred feet higher than the surrounding forest, the big pines thrived only in areas where they were tucked into the landscape, protected from wind throw and lightning strikes. Steep-sided ravines and riparian sites backed by tall river terraces were the realm of these giants.

Three hundred years ago sugar maple and beech, not pine, most likely dominated the area surrounding the trail, because prior to British settlement white pines were restricted to either sandy substrates of valley bottoms or rocky substrates of ridgetops. Their presence suggests that the landscape I walk through was altered by human activity. Stone walls running through this pine woodland and old, wide-spreading sugar maples speak of abandoned pastures. The rocks incorporated into the walls I pass are schists that look like dark slate with surface ripples, but large square chunks of white granite hint at the changes to come.

Soon a ledge to the left of the trail rises abruptly—the first outcropping of granite. As I continue, the granite outcrop approaches the trail at an acute angle, and with a single step I pass from an underlayment of schist to one of granite. The resulting change in vegetation is profound: Rich-sited herbs, such as baneberry, are replaced with dense thickets of mountain laurel—a broad-leaved, evergreen shrub that is a member of the heath family.

Mountain laurel

The laurel is unique among Vermont's woody plants with its large, waxy, evergreen leaves. This attribute restricts the mountain laurel to warm sites in the southern part of the state. It's not the cold itself that's a problem for the laurel's large leaves, but the low relative humidity associated with frigid winter nights. When temperatures reach minus fifteen degrees Fahrenheit, the air is so dry that the laurel's leaves desiccate, killing the shrub. Given this risk to its survival, why would the laurel keep its large leaves all winter instead of shedding them the way all the other regional woodland trees and shrubs do? By keeping its leaves, the plant is able to conduct the majority of its annual photosynthesis in October, November, March, and April while the forest canopy is devoid of foliage. This allows the mountain laurel to do two things our other native woodland shrubs can't—reach large size and produce an opulent bloom.

It's the reason I have chosen this evening, four days after the summer solstice, for a walk up Black Mountain—the mountain laurel is in full bloom. Its white flowers cover the shrubs, making the understory look as if it's been blanketed in snow. No other shrub in the forests of New England can create such a rich floral display, one whose white blooms will guide me down the trail well after dark.

The mountain laurel on Black Mountain is the northernmost population of this species in Vermont's Connecticut River Valley. Here at the northern extreme of its range it is restricted not only to warm sites, but to acidic sites as well, where competitors can't thrive. Granite bedrock weathers into very acidic soils. Yet if we were to travel into the heart of the mountain laurel's range—say, the Great

Smoky Mountains—we'd find it dominating the understories of rich, moist-sited forests. Not so in Vermont: When species reach their maximum range limits, they often seek out extreme sites to avoid resident competitors.

Above the laurel, red oaks and white pines dominate the forest canopy. Like the laurel, these trees tolerate acidic, dry sites. I know from previous trips to Black Mountain that I will pass through two more distinct pine-dominated communities during my hike to the summit, the first composed of red pine, white oak, and black huckleberry and the second a mix of pitch pine, bear oak, and low-bush blueberry.

The trail turns to the left and the laurel thickens to an almost impenetrable head-high wall on each side of the trail. Soon red pines replace red oaks and white pines as the dominant canopy trees, and scattered white oaks grow here and there. The mountain laurel is thinning as well and is replaced by black huckleberry, another member of the heath family. All three of these new species indicate that conditions are becoming drier and more acidic.

I ascend a north-facing ramp toward the summit that is very consistent in its pitch—a hill-climbing grade that would be suitable for cars. Exposed granite ledge becomes more and more prevalent, now rivaling black huckleberry as the most common feature of the forest understory. As I crest the summit, I break through the canopy of red pine and into a landscape of scattered, gnarled pitch pines and bushy bear oaks. The black huckleberry gives way to low-bush blueberry.

During my hike up Black Mountain the amount of exposed granite ledge has steadily increased. Now smooth expanses of white, rounded granite cover more than half the summit area around me. As I stand here, *White Mountain* seems like a more appropriate name, but I'm guessing that from a distance the exposed summit bedrock is less visible than the dark forests of pine that cloak the mountain's slopes. The granite gently swoops and rolls across the summit, looking as if it has been worked with a giant wood gouge and then sanded

Bear oak twig

smooth. This is very different from the rougher, exposed metamorphic ledges that I've seen on the surrounding ridgetops. I stoop to touch the granite; sections of it feel as smooth as glass. There are few fractures on its surface, but numerous depressions, filled with coarse sands produced by the weathering of the bedrock, support rock-garden-like beds of haircap moss, reindeer lichen, and low-bush blueberry. Scattered above these are widely spaced, multiple-stemmed bear oaks no more than five feet in height, each laden with the bullet-sized acorns so prized by its namesake. Because of the tree's small stature and the numerous acorns that cling to its branches, a bear can run its teeth over a branch and get a mouthful of acorns in one pass. Above the oaks are twisting pitch pines, whose trunks, covered in tufts of needles, make these irregularly shaped trees seem even scruffier. As I cross the summit to the south, the smooth, rolling granite gives way to a much more angular face, and the bedrock descends in a steep set of stairs suitable only for a giant's stride.

I am now standing on the harshest, hottest, and driest site in all Vermont. The open, steep, south-facing slope of granite receives more solar radiation and holds less moisture than anywhere else in the state, making it the only place in Vermont where bear oak grows. And yet with a slight evening breeze, the exposed dome of granite feels anything but inhospitable. The views from this expansive, bald summit are framed by the unique twisting branches of pitch pines. The smooth exposed granite beckons me to sit, and it holds the warmth of the day as the evening descends around me.

All the features I have described here, from the mountain laurels up to the summit views, are classic attributes of the granite domes of the northern United States. All granite domes, whether they occur in the high Sierra, the Rockies, or the mountains of the Northeast, host gnarled pines, depression communities often dominated by heaths, and expanses of smooth, undulating light-colored granite. The bedrock itself dictates these similarities and creates landscapes that feel very different from other exposed, bedrock summits—landscapes that draw me time and again with their austere beauty. In fact, given the choice, I'll hike a granite bald over any other kind of open summit. Such is the power of exposed granite.

Although you'll find granite domes throughout North America, this book focuses on balds that have been sculpted by glacial ice—those occurring in our northern states. In the Southeast a few granite domes exist—Stone Mountain in Georgia being a fine example—but they are rare. Granite domes are common in the Southwest, but the hot, dry climate weathers them by breaking up their surface. I find smooth expanses of bedrock to be the most compelling, and only the glacially scoured granites of our northern mountains have this quality—in some instances creating floors of bedrock, completely devoid of cracks, larger than a football field.

To truly understand and appreciate these unique mountain domes, there are certain things we need to know: why granite is distinct among rocks; how it is created; why all mountains have a granite core; why granite weathers to form smooth, rounded domes, how plants colonize these harsh, dry, acidic environments; and how disturbance perpetually keeps these domes open and exposed. By examining the origins of granite, glaciation, outcrop succession, and the role of disturbance, the four chapters of part One lay the geological and ecological foundations for the features that are common to all exposed granite domes. Part Two then explores the particular natural history of granite domes found in the various mountain ranges in our northern states.

I imagine many of you reading this book have already strode over expansive, glacially scoured floors of granite, but may have given little thought to how your experience hiking on this bedrock differs from that on other mountainous landscapes. As with my previous book, *Reading the Forested Landscape,* which helps people see forests in new ways by unraveling their histories through tangible clues, my aim with this book is to open your eyes to the unique attributes found on granite domes. But unlike forested landscapes, whose histories are measured in centuries, the forces that have shaped domes of granite involve the deep time of mountain building and the slow work of ice, wind, fire, lichen, and heath. By gaining a deeper understanding of what makes granite domes look and feel as they do, it is my hope that you will experience these compelling landscapes in new and exciting ways.

PART ONE

THE MAKING OF GRANITE DOMES

Granite with glacial boulders, Yosemite National Park

CHAPTER ONE

Origins of Granite

Whenever I pass a cemetery while driving through Vermont, I can guess the date of its origin and whether or not it remains in use simply by looking at the composition of its gravestones. Just as an abandoned meadow will proceed from herbs to shrubs to trees, cemeteries show a clearly defined sequence in their headstones. Prior to 1810 all the region's gravestones were slate, which was easily quarried and inscribed. However, the same feature that made slate easy to quarry—its regular flat bedding planes—also gave it an undesirable quality as a gravestone: Its inscribed surface could simply cleave off from the rest of the stone. So early in the 1800s slate headstones were replaced by marble, another stone that was easy to cut and inscribe. But inscriptions on marble were eroded by rainfall, which is slightly acidic, so by 1890 marble gravestones gave way to durable granite—the rock of ages.

The next chance you get, closely examine some granite. How would you describe its appearance? It's a light-colored rock—either white, gray, or orange pink—and is composed of fairly large, easily discernible crystals. This coarse, crystalline structure gave granite its name, from the Latin *granum* (meaning "grain"). Looking more closely, you will see that the largest and most common crystals are also responsible for granite's overall white, gray, or pink color. These crystals are feldspar, which comprises 50 to 70 percent of the granite by volume. The next most common crystal is quartz, at 25 to 40 percent. The least common, at 3 to 10

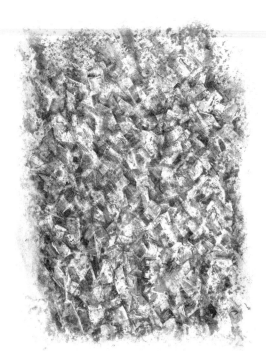

Closeup of the mineral texture of granite

percent, are dark, iron-containing minerals, usually either mica or hornblende. It is the feldspar and quartz—two of the hardest minerals commonly found in rock—that make granite so durable. Although the stone is much harder to carve than marble or slate, inscriptions on granite gravestones will last for millennia.

There are many rocks with properties quite similar to granite—tonalite, granodiorite, quartz monzonite—whose mineral compositions vary somewhat from the above percentages. For the purposes of this book, *granite* will refer to any coarse-grained, igneous rock whose most common minerals are feldspar and quartz, in that order.

TYPES OF ROCK

Geologists have categorized rock into three major groups: *sedimentary, metamorphic,* and *igneous*. Sedimentary rock is often formed from layers of silt or sand—eroded and carried away from previously existing bedrock—that have cemented together to form new rocks such as shale or sandstone. If sedimentary rocks are subjected to heat and pressure below the Earth's surface, they may partially melt to form metamorphic rocks like slate or quartzite. Igneous rocks arise from the cooling of *magma*—rock that has been heated until it melts into liquid deep within the Earth's crust.

If the magma surfaces in a volcanic eruption, it will cool quickly to form what are called extrusive igneous rocks, such as lava. Magma that cools underground creates intrusive igneous rocks. The slower the cooling of magma, the larger the resulting mineral grains of the rock. Extrusive igneous rocks cool so quickly that they don't display a granular texture. But granite always forms as an intrusive rock many miles below the surface of the Earth; there it cools slowly, creating its coarse-grained texture. Slow-cooling, coarse-grained granites have mineral crystals larger than a centimeter in width, but even fine-grained granites have crystals up to half a centimeter.

Again examine your granite closely. Which are the most perfectly formed crystals? It's the dark crystals, the mica or hornblend, that cool and crystallize first and therefore aren't confined by surrounding mineral grains. The feldspars solidify next, again creating well-formed crystals with smooth surfaces. But quartz, the last mineral to crystallize, is confined between hardened grains of feldspar and mica or hornblend, and as such can't produce perfectly shaped crystals. This process of crystallization is similar to the frost that forms on windows in cold climates. With unlimited space frost can form well-defined, intricate, feathery plumes, analogous to the nicely shaped crystals of mica, hornblend, and feldspar. But when confined, the crystalline structure loses its regular form to become a jumble of irregular polygons. This is what happens to quartz.

All the granite domes we stride across today were once pools of liquid rock trapped many miles below the Earth's surface. To go further back and understand how rock becomes molten and how granite is created deep underground, we need to delve into the realm of *plate tectonics*—arguably the single most important theory developed in geological science.

Plate tectonic theory describes the Earth's crust as being composed of about a dozen large, rigid sections called plates that slowly move across the globe's surface. Intense heat within the Earth drives the movement of the plates, much the way heat generated on the surface of our planet causes air masses to move across the globe. These plates separate at *rifting zones* and collide along other portions of their margins. When the denser oceanic crust of one plate collides with the lighter continental crust of another plate, the oceanic crust is slowly forced beneath the continental crust in a process called *subduction*. The crust plunges down into the Earth's internal furnace and melts to become magma. The molten rock, having a

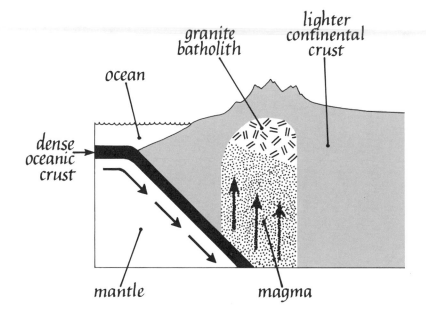

lower density, then slowly migrates up toward the Earth's surface, creating uplift and mountain building. If the magma breaks the surface, a volcano is born. Magma that gets trapped and solidifies miles below the surface cools slowly to form granite.

PLATE TECTONICS

If you have a map of the world, take a look at the continents that border the Atlantic Ocean, particularly North America, South America, and Africa. If you cut these continents out of the map and placed South America alongside Africa, they would fit together pretty tightly, with Senegal in western Africa lying adjacent to eastern Venezuela. If you then brought the eastern seaboard of the United States in contact with the upper coast of western Africa, it would fit nicely as well. This is exactly what Alfred Wegener, a German meteorologist, did early in the twentieth century. From this and the shapes and arrangement of other continents, he hypothesized in 1912 that all of the Earth's landmasses were once assembled into a single supercontinent he named Pangaea (translated as "all-earth"), which had subsequently broken up and drifted apart. His *continental drift* hypothesis was not based solely on the matching shapes of continents but was also supported by geological and biological evidence.

His strongest evidence came from South America and Africa. Wegener noted the way mountain chains and bedrock formations lined up when these continents were placed side by side. The most striking correlation occurred between similar unusual mineral-bearing bedrock formations found in Brazil and South Africa that lined up perfectly when the continental puzzle pieces were fitted together. He also recognized the similarities between fossils and living organisms of the two continents, including the kinship between the South American rheas and African ostriches—both large, flightless birds. As Chet and Maureen Raymo write in their wonderful book *Written in Stone,* "Not only did the shape of the puzzle pieces match, but also the picture on the puzzle." As powerful as Wegener's evidence was, his hypothesis had a fatal flaw: He couldn't explain how continents could migrate across the surface of the Earth.

Wegener knew that continental bedrock is less dense, and therefore lighter, than the rock that forms the oceans' floors. He imagined the lighter continents floating upon the denser oceanic rock like boats in the water, and like boats they could be propelled through the seas. But oceanic rock was solid, not liquid, so what force could propel continents through it? Without a viable answer to this question, Wegener's hypothesis of continental drift was rejected by the scientific community to lie dormant for half a century.

Technological developments expand the boundaries of science by allowing us to perceive things hidden to our unaided senses. Although a dark period in human history, World War II was a fountainhead for new technologies, not all of them created for destruction. With the invention of sonar, the topography of the oceans' floors could finally be "seen."

Ships carrying troops were outfitted with fathometers to monitor ocean depth when approaching beachheads. One of the commanders of these ships was Harry Hess, a geologist by training. Hess realized that if he kept his fathometer on during ocean crossings, he could begin to map the contour of the ocean floor, which at the time was thought to be flat. To his surprise he found not only numerous isolated *seamounts* but also mid-oceanic ridges that seemed to stretch for hundreds of miles. In addition, these ridges were cleft, as if their crests had been cut down lengthwise by a massive knife.

As the seafloors of the world were mapped following World War II, similar ridge systems were found in all the Earth's oceans. In 1962 Hess assembled the existing ocean-floor data and used them as the basis of his theory of *seafloor spreading*. He proposed that the oceanic ridge systems were in fact rifting zones (explaining their cleft nature) where the ocean crust was constantly opening up to allow lava to surface and form new crust. The production of new crust pushed the existing oceanic floor on each side of the rift farther apart, resulting in seafloor spreading.

But like Wegener's, Hess's theory was not well received. If in fact the ocean floors were spreading, geologists wondered, then why wasn't the surface of the Earth expanding? Hess responded that the oceanic crust was being reabsorbed into the Earth along the margins of the deep ocean trenches lying adjacent to continental shelves (much like the functioning of an escalator), keeping the surface of the Earth in a state of equilibrium. Without corroborating physical evidence to support seafloor spreading or the subduction of oceanic crust into deep sea trenches, however, the scientific community was not prepared to accept Hess's theory.

Then a few years later two new pieces of evidence came to light to support Hess. Geologists began to examine the oceanic crust through deep-sea drilling. They knew that as magma solidifies, iron-containing minerals in the rock line themselves up with the Earth's magnetic field. When examined in terms of their magnetic alignments, samples of oceanic crust extracted along a transect between Europe and North America generated an astounding finding: Our Earth's magnetic field has completely reversed itself numerous times during its history. What is now the North Pole was the South Pole just a few million years ago. This finding provided strong evidence to support seafloor spreading, for on both sides of the *Mid-Atlantic Ridge* (a cleft ridge thousands of miles long that mimics the bends of the continental shorelines on both sides of the Atlantic) the patterns of paleomagnetic reversals were a mirror image. If the mid-Atlantic rift indeed opened and lava surfaced to form new oceanic crust, the orientation of the iron-containing minerals on both sides of the rift would be the same. Then, when a reversal in the Earth's magnetic field occurred, the newly formed crust on both sides of the rift would record it, creating the same pattern of reversals in the oceanic crust on both sides of the Mid-Atlantic Ridge.

Shortly after this discovery, analysis of the age of the oceanic crust showed that whereas close to the Mid-Atlantic Ridge it was very young, it grew progressively older as it approached either North America or Europe; further, the crust adjacent to each of the continental margins was of similar age. With these new discoveries, the geological world was sent into turmoil as numerous old theories were jettisoned and replaced by a single, new theory that incorporated both Wegener's continental drift and Hess's seafloor spreading. This new theory, plate tectonics, describes the surface of the Earth as a patchwork of about a dozen large plates and numerous smaller ones (many containing both continental and oceanic crust) delineated by rifting and subduction zones. The elegance of plate tectonics is that it explains such dramatically different geological events as earthquakes, volcanic eruptions, mountain building, and even the evolution of life in one unifying theory. It also helps us understand how new rock, including granite, comes into being.

THE EARTH'S ANATOMY

The Earth's crust—analogous to the shell of an egg—is composed of solid rock that is only a few miles thick under the ocean basins but tens of miles thick under continental mountain ranges. This analogy is useful because the thickness of an egg's shell in relation to the whole egg is similar to the thickness of the Earth's crust in relation to the whole planet.

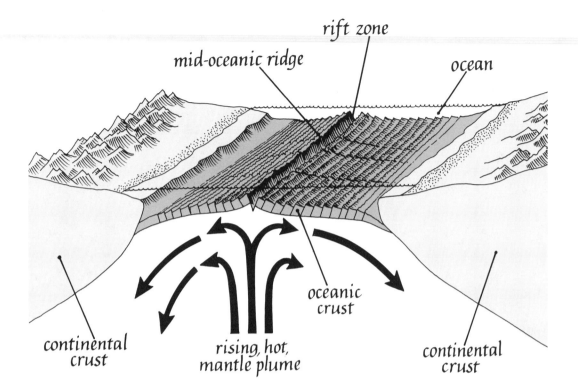

rift zone

mid-oceanic ridge

ocean

oceanic crust

continental crust

rising, hot, mantle plume

continental crust

Beneath the crust, representing the bulk of the volume of the Earth, is the *mantle*—analogous to the egg white. The mantle is composed of material in a physical state somewhere between solid and liquid, namely plastic. Like solids, plastics have form, but like liquids they flow and change their form given enough time. Silly Putty, a toy developed during my childhood, is a fine example of a plastic. We can roll it into a ball, but if we let it sit on a table, the ball slowly flows to take on the appearance of a pancake.

The mantle surrounds the Earth's core—the yolk of the egg. The core is composed of molten iron and a lot of radioactive elements, which produce intense heat deep within the Earth as they decay. The heat drives convection cells in the Earth's mantle, which rise in certain portions of the globe until they collide with the crust. Not being able to punch through the solid crust, the mantle is diverted laterally underneath it. As the mantle plume diverges left and right under the crust, it stretches the surface, tearing it open and creating rifting zones such as the Mid-Atlantic Ridge. The mantle slowly cools and becomes denser as it travels beneath the crust and then sinks back toward the core, only to be heated once again to rise in the mantle plume. If you'd like to see a similar process, heat some water to boiling in a pot, then throw in some oats. Watch as the oats rise in the center, separate, and then sink toward the bottom, only to cycle again. The major difference between oats' and the mantle's convection cells is time. While the oats take about a second to complete their cycle, the mantle takes tens of millions of years.

It is the heating and rising of mantle below the Earth's crust that causes plates to divide along rift zones and to collide at other portions of their boundaries. Whenever the continental crust of one plate collides with the continental crust of another plate, mountains are built. This is occurring right now in the Himalayas, where the plate carrying India is plowing into mainland Asia. Such a mountain range has limited volcanic activity, because the continental crust of each plate is too light to be forced down into the Earth, where it could be heated to the melting point. Instead, it crumples upward like the hoods of two cars involved in a head-on collision.

However, when oceanic crust from one plate collides with continental crust from another plate, volcanic activity commonly accompanies mountain building. Being denser, the oceanic crust is subducted beneath the lighter continental crust. Heated to melting, it expands and pushes its way toward the surface as magma, sometimes erupting as a volcano but often solidifying below as intrusive igneous rock that warps the continental crust upward into a range of mountains.

The composition of the magma determines the nature of volcanic activity and the kinds of intrusive igneous rock formed by subduction. And the composition of the subducted crust determines the composition of the magma. The crust that lies beneath the oceans is basaltic in composition. *Basalt* is a dense rock heavy with iron and magnesium. When basaltic crust melts, it creates very fluid magma that often surfaces in volcanic eruptions with extensive lava flows and little volcanic ash. The eruptions witnessed on the Hawaiian Islands, with their lava fountains and ample flows, are classic examples of the work of basaltic magma.

At the other end of the spectrum are *rhyolitic magmas,* which are formed from light continental crust that is rich in silicates. Rhyolitic magma is viscous and also has water as one of its constituents. When it surfaces, it creates violent eruptions as the water expands to steam, blasting the magma into small particles of ash, cinders, or pumice. Mount St. Helens is a classic example of the release of rhyolitic magma. Since two-thirds of the composition of granite is in the form of silicates (major components of quartz and feldspar minerals), we know it is derived from rhyolitic magma that never surfaces and solidifies many miles below the Earth's crust.

But if it is the basaltic oceanic crust that is forced down to form magma when two plates collide, how are rhyolitic magmas formed? The answer is that the oceanic crust drags a large amount of the colliding continental crust with it. So much so that in areas where oceanic crust is subducted beneath continental crust, extrusive volcanic material is usually only about one-tenth the volume of the granites that are formed deep within the evolving mountain chain. This means that any mountain range formed when oceanic crust is subducted below continental crust—including the Sierra Nevada and the Andes—has at its deepest roots a huge bed of granite. These beds often involve areas larger than a thousand square kilometers, but whenever they are greater than a hundred square kilometers, they are called *batholiths* (meaning "deep rock"). Every mountain range discussed in this book is the remnant of an ancient granite batholith whose original mountains were long ago carried to the sea.

The next time you find yourself on a dome of granite, contemplate that roughly ten miles of crustal bedrock has been removed through erosion to expose the batholith on which you stand. Also consider that geologically speaking, mountain ranges are exceedingly short lived. It takes only five million years to build a range such as the Himalayas, and about the same amount of time for erosion to deposit them in the ocean. But granite batholiths have much greater longevity: They can easily exist a hundred times longer than the mountains to which they gave birth. "The rock of ages" is indeed an apt title for granite.

Glacially scoured granite on Champlain Mountain, Acadia National Park

CHAPTER TWO

Sculpted by Glaciers

I'm perched on an unnamed dome seven hundred feet above Yosemite's Tuolumne River. The granite beneath my feet is perfectly smooth and almost white in color, but about twenty feet to my right the smooth surface becomes pockmarked, looking like a wall from which patches of plaster have fallen. To my left the smooth surface is cut by a series of long, parallel, straight lines, and farther away a broad trough runs in the same direction. In front of me the dome gracefully sweeps upward, and then drops abruptly toward the river. This dome is one in a series that lines both sides of the Tuolumne. Each displays features similar to the one on which I sit. Looking up and beyond the river valley, I see many more domes rising into the southeastern highlands a few miles distant, their white crowns in stark contrast to the dark green forests of pine and red fir that enshroud their bases.

It is a land of granite, a landscape of antiquity. Like all the domelands covered in this book, the exposed granite here is more than one hundred million years old—formed in the belly of the ancestral Sierra Nevada, miles below the surface of the Earth. Yet I sit close to two miles above sea level. Ancient erosion removed miles of overlying bedrock to expose this granite, and geologically recent uplift generated by the subduction of the Pacific Plate has raised it to this height. To really know this Yosemite landscape (as well as the others covered in this book) and all the features I see from my perch, it's essential to understand glaciation and the sculpted features created by glacial ice. But before delving into the past workings of glacial ice, let's first examine two other forces currently responsible for eroding granite domes in America today.

EXFOLIATION AND SPHEROIDAL WEATHERING

The exposed granite that I see in Yosemite differs in one important way from its original state underground. Once miles of overlying bedrock were removed through erosion, a dramatic release of compressive pressure on the granite allowed the rock to expand. In the process of expanding, the granite developed a series of curvilinear fractures called *expansion joints*. The best way to visualize the arrangement of these expansion joints is to imagine an onion cut into quarters. If you held one of the quarters, you'd see the curved layers of the onion, each layer thinner than the last, as you moved toward the outer surface. This arrangement is what we would find if we could slice a granite dome from top to bottom—a series of curved sections of granite that get thinner as we move toward the surface of the dome. The thinnest surficial sections may be a couple of feet thick, while deep within a granite dome the sections can be many dozens of feet thick.

When water seeps into the fractures of a rock and freezes, the resulting expansion of the ice can cleave off sections of the rock. A major reason why granite is more resistant to erosion than sedimentary and metamorphic rocks is that it has far fewer surficial crevices. Yet on cliff faces and the steep sides of domes, large chunks of granite can be cleaved off along their expansion joints. The process is called *exfoliation*.

A few years back my next-door neighbor David Walter, an avid rock climber, witnessed a dramatic exfoliation event in Yosemite Valley. David was climbing Royal Arches the evening of July 10, 1996, when a thirty-foot-thick slab of granite, estimated at eighty thousand tons, broke loose and launched off Washburn Point—about a mile from where David was climbing. The slab underwent a seventeen-hundred-foot vertical free fall, remaining intact until it hit the valley floor at an estimated speed of 160 miles an hour. On contact the slab particalized

A granite ledge dissected by expansion joints

to dust and produced a sound similar to a sonic boom. David caught the entire sequence on his camera as the resulting dust cloud grew to fill the valley. The compressed air from the slab's impact leveled about ten acres of forest near the Happy Isles Nature Center and stripped the bark from trees three hundred feet away. David had the luck to witness and photograph an event that is rare in the span of a human lifetime—but not in the lifespan of a granite dome. In a place like Yosemite exfoliations of this magnitude happen each century.

Since the expansion joints are curved in granite, the exfoliation of surficial sections naturally creates steep-sided dome-shaped structures. Following glaciation, exfoliation is one of the the major ways by which granite mountains weather away. In hot dry climates, however, *spheroidal weathering* is the major agent in the erosion of granite domes.

Spheroidal weathering is the direct result of granite being composed of large grains of different minerals. Each of those minerals expands and contracts at a slightly different rate as the granite is heated during the day and cooled at night. Because of these different expansion and contraction rates, the minerals in the rock start to lever each other apart. This happens more quickly on surface irregularities, edges, and along joints that have a larger amount of surface area in relationship to their volume, and as a result expand and contract more than smooth portions of the granite. Over time surface irregularities are removed and the granite erodes into spherical boulders—a shape that has the least amount of surface area in relationship to its volume. In hot, dry climates the daily expansion and contraction of granite is very pronounced, and spheroidal weathering is common.

Every other year in March I co-lead a desert ecology course for Antioch New England Graduate School. Most recently we ventured to the central desert of Baja Mexico. In the region around the town of Catavina, the process of spheroidal weathering is dramatic. The granite batholith that underlies much of Baja lies exposed. Here huge, round granite boulders lie on top of one another, creating intriguing formations reminiscent of the work of

Andy Goldsworthy, a sculptor who uses materials from nature. It's easy to imagine giants at work here, yet the sculptor is the desert climate, and its medium is granite ledge.

Since granite erodes rapidly through spheroidal weathering in regions with hot, dry climates, smooth expanses are rare—which is why this book examines only domes found in northern states, where the granite is much sturdier and able to form extensive hard, smooth surfaces. Although exfoliation plays an important role in our northern domes, the number one factor responsible for their present physical appearance is glaciation.

GLACIATION

At the ridge crest to the southeast from where I sit in Yosemite lies Lyell Glacier. I know this only because it's labeled on my map; looking at it from this distance, I can't tell if it's a glacier or just a snowfield. So if these two mountain features look so similar, what distinguishes a glacier from a snowfield? The difference lies in the depth of accumulated snow that has been compressed into ice.

A glacier is formed when compressed ice reaches depths of more than sixty meters. The sheer weight of this much frozen water crushes the precise molecular structure of the ice at the bottom of the glacier, forcing water molecules closer together. The result is that the ice is transformed from a solid into a plastic—a substance that does have form but can also slowly flow and change its shape. Because of the plastic nature of a glacier, the pull of gravity makes it flow over the land (something a static snowfield can't do), dramatically sculpting the landscape as it moves.

As the glacial ice flows, it first scrapes off the soil, and then the bedrock. The ice at the bottom of the glacier becomes loaded with clay, silt, sand, gravel, and rocks of all sizes. These materials increase the glacier's ability to erode the land, turning it into a huge sanding device with a power beyond imagination, as it slowly—but completely—refinishes the surface of all the terrain it encounters.

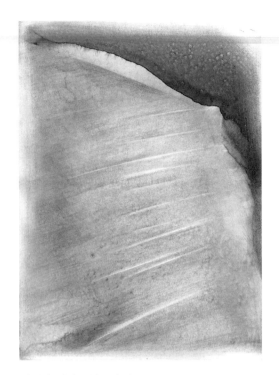
Glacial polish with striations

Geologists distinguish between two basic types of glacier—continental and alpine. Continental glaciers are huge ice sheets that cover entire or large portions of a continent, the ice sheets on Greenland and Antarctica being examples. Generally, continental glaciers grind down the surfaces of huge areas of the globe and leave in their wake landscapes with greatly reduced relief. Alpine glaciers are restricted to mountainous terrain and carve their way into the sides of mountains, dramatically accentuating relief. In the eastern United States a continental glacier created the granite domes covered in this book, whereas alpine glaciers that merged and covered large areas of mountain terrain—in Yosemite everything between eight and ten thousand feet—created the bald domes of the West.

Whether alpine or continental, glacial ice works on granite in the same fashion and develops a number of characteristic erosional features. The smooth surface on which I sit is called *glacial polish*. It's created by the clays, silts, and fine sands that are trapped in the ice. Like a fine-grit sandpaper rubbed over wood, the glacier polishes the granite surface to a mirror-smooth finish. The most extensive glacial polish I've encountered occurs in Yosemite, with some areas as large as football fields and almost as smooth as ice. At the top of this dome the polish covers an area roughly sixty feet in diameter. Farther out, portions of the polish have eroded away, creating rough depressions about a centimeter deep. Although extensive glacial polish such as this is uncommon in other regions of the country, wherever there is glaciated granite, remnants of it can be found. The next time you find yourself on glaciated granite, take a moment

Chatter marks

to bend down and slide your hand across these remnants. You are feeling a bedrock surface that has remained virtually unchanged for ten thousand years or more!

On softer granites, straight parallel scratches can sometimes be seen etched into the surface, such as those to my left. These *glacial striations,* always pointing in the direction of the glacial flow, are left from small hard rocks embedded in the bottom of the ice sheet that were scraped over the granite, cutting into its polished surface. To my far left an embedded boulder carved out a similar but larger feature called a *glacial groove.* After it was cut, this large trough was polished smooth. Glacial grooves are wider than they are deep, in widths of two to more than ten feet.

This dome lacks a feature that is often seen on glaciated granite, a series of crescent-shaped depressions formed when the glacier removed flakes of granite. But how could ice latch on to smooth bedrock and chip out flakes? The glacial ice couldn't, but an embedded boulder

Roche moutonnée

could. In this instance the boulder wasn't dragged across the granite in a smooth, continuous motion but was repeatedly pushed down into the bedrock, acting like a giant, slow-motion jackhammer. When they occur in a series, these depressions are called *chatter marks*. The size of the crescents directly related to the size of the boulder that made them. The next time you encounter chatter marks, approximate the size of the boulder that made them by completing the imaginary circle inferred by the crescent. The bulge of these crescents points in the direction the boulder skipped across the granite—the direction of glacial flow. I see glacial polish, striations, and grooves at my feet, but some other erosional features occur at larger spatial scales and can be observed only from a distance.

In front of me the polished granite gently sweeps up a distance of fifty feet and then drops an abrupt ten feet. On this almost vertical face the granite is anything but smooth, resembling a series of steep, irregular steps. The graceful incline looks similar to the smooth line of a whale's back and is so named. Together the whaleback and steep irregular face form a glacially eroded feature called a *roche moutonnée* (stone sheep), because the form reminded French geologists of sheep reposing in pastures. Since glacial ice acts as a huge sanding device, why does it sculpt roche moutonnées instead of just leveling granite outcrops?

As a glacier rides over a granite outcropping, it slowly sands the whaleback smooth. When the ice is forced up and over the granite outcropping, the compressive pressure within the glacier is increased, melting the ice that is in contact with the rock. The meltwater seeps into horizontal cracks in the bedrock (called joints) and refreezes as the pressure is released. This allows the glacier to grab on to large chunks of granite and pull them away as it continues its flow, quarrying a steep rock face.

Looking out to the farthest domes in the southeast, I can see that some of them are separated by deep U-shaped valleys called *glacial notches*. When glacial ice is forced to flow in a valley between existing outcroppings of bedrock, the compressive forces increase and the valley is dramatically cut into a deep U shape. On the top of a granite outcrop glaciers may sand-away several feet of bedrock, but this is minor compared to the hundreds of feet of rock they may carve out of a valley.

There is one last feature common to glaciated granite domes. When chunks of bedrock are quarried from outcroppings by a glacier, they are tumbled in slow motion within the ice, over time becoming more rounded. When glaciers melt away, all the materials trapped in their ice—clays, sands, gravels, and larger boulders—are released. Meltwater and gravity carry most of these materials off a granite dome, but boulders too big to be moved stay where they were deposited. If a glacial boulder is a different type of rock than the bedrock on which it sits, it's called a *glacial erratic*. More than two hundred years ago ridgetop erratics in Europe were used as scientific proof of catastrophic biblical floods. But in 1840 Louis Agassiz, a brilliant Swiss scientist, showed not only that the erratics were left by glaciers but, more importantly, that much of Europe had at one time been covered by glacial ice. Agassiz is renowned for his many accomplishments, but certainly a critical one was developing the study of glacial geology and giving rise to the notion of ice ages.

The granite on which I sit—indeed, all Yosemite—looks the way it does because the Earth is in the midst of an ice age. Considering that the only ice visible from my vantage point lies in the Lyell Glacier, it seems hard to believe this, but from a global perspective an ice age is a period when the Earth's average annual temperature is decreased and ice sheets cover at least one of its poles. These two conditions currently exist, placing us in the third major ice age since the beginning of the Cambrian period almost six hundred million years ago. The two previous ice ages commenced 450 million years ago during the Ordovician period, and 350 million years ago during the Carboniferous period. Our present ice age began about forty million years ago with the development of the Antarctic Ice Sheet. But since the Cambrian, only during the past two million years—the Pleistocene epoch—have continental glaciers covered large landmasses in both hemispheres, making this an unusual time in the Earth's history. At times during the Pleistocene, ice sheets on North America and Eurasia have dwarfed those on Antarctica and Greenland, making this epoch our most intense period of global glaciation during the past six hundred million years. All the granite domes covered in this book are the result of Pleistocene glaciations.

PLEISTOCENE GLACIATIONS

In order for an ice age to begin, it appears necessary to have either a thermally isolated continent such as Antarctica (surrounded by ocean) or a thermally isolated ocean such as the Arctic Ocean (surrounded by land) residing at a pole—a condition that has existed on Earth for at least forty million years. To birth continental glaciers—such as the one Agassiz determined had covered much of Europe—it is necessary to have continents at high latitudes. This condition has also existed in the Northern Hemisphere since the onset of our current ice age. So why did the development of continental glaciers in North America and Eurasia commence only two million years ago rather than forty million? For the birth of a continental glacier, something else is needed in addition to its position at high latitudes—a source of moisture-rich air. A distinct change had to occur in the global system to introduce more moisture into the higher latitudes of the Northern Hemisphere.

For millions of years South America and North America were not connected by Central America. During this time a warm equatorial current flowed from the Atlantic Ocean directly into the Pacific. But three million years ago, due to plate tectonic activity, the Isthmus of Panama formed, linking the Americas. The warm equatorial current was deflected northward to become the Gulf Stream—a conveyor belt of moist warm air flowing directly into the heart of the Arctic.

At the same time India, which had been drifting northward for millions of years, slammed into Asia. The collision of these two continental plates created the Himalayas. This most massive of mountain ranges has altered circulation patterns in the atmosphere of the entire globe, possibly deflecting more moisture to northern latitudes as well. With these events large continental glaciers grew to cover much of North America and Eurasia and alpine glaciers cloaked many of the Earth's mountain ranges. But where are those glaciers today if we are in the midst of an ice age?

We don't know much about the specifics of the Ordovician or Carboniferous ice ages, but we have strong evidence to suggest that the current Pleistocene epoch has been characterized by a dizzying cycle of glaciations, each followed by a short interglacial period when global climates dramatically warm and glaciers in the Northern Hemisphere rapidly disappear. It is within the most recent interglacial, the Holocene epoch, that we presently find ourselves. Not only has there been a glacial-interglacial cycle, but the cycle for the past million years has been quite consistent in its timing. The past eight glaciations have each lasted about one hundred thousand years, with all the succeeding interglacials lasting about ten thousand years. What could be responsible for such a regular cycle? The strongest theory suggests that celestial events are the perpetrators.

Contrary to popular belief, the Earth doesn't revolve around the sun in a regular, set pattern. Three irregularities in its orbit influence global climates and the onset of interglacial periods. In this theory glaciation is the norm, with interglacials occurring approximately every hundred thousand years when a particular alignment is reached between Earth and sun — the result of the irregular orbital movements.

If the Earth were alone in its orbit around the sun, its movement would be steady and consistent. The Pleistocene would in all likelihood have been characterized by continuous glaciation, and I wouldn't be writing this book in Vermont (which would be covered by more than a mile of glacial ice). In fact, there would probably be no books, since humans might have continued to exist solely as hunter-gatherers. It's believed that this present interglacial most likely sparked the development of agriculture, which eventually gave rise to industrial culture. But the moon and neighboring planets tug on the Earth, creating the irregularities I'll explain.

The first of these eccentricities relates to the Earth's orbit around the sun, which goes from almost circular to elliptical and then back to circular every hundred thousand years. It is important to note that the sun is offset from the center of the Earth's orbit; when the orbit is most elliptical, the sun is most off-center. The second irregularity relates to the tilt of the Earth's axis in relation to its orbit. The tilt reaches a maximum of 24.5 degrees and a minimum of 22 degrees. It is predominantly the gravitational pulls of Venus and Jupiter working together that create this forty-one-thousand-year cycle from maximal tilt to minimal tilt and back. Finally, the last eccentricity is a wobble in the tilt of the Earth's axis, similar to what we would observe in a spinning top that begins to slow down. The gravitational pulls of the moon and the sun cause the Earth, while it is spinning on its axis, to make one complete turn in its axial tilt every twenty-two thousand years. The importance of the wobble is that it determines during what season the Earth is physically closest to the sun. Presently the Earth is closest to the sun during our Northern Hemisphere's winter (winter occurs when the tilt of the Earth's axis is pointing away from the sun, not when the Earth is farthest from the sun). Yet because of the wobble, eleven thousand years ago we were closest to the sun during our Northern Hemisphere's summer. The Northern Hemisphere is critical because this is where the bulk of high-latitude landmasses lie—places that can birth huge continental glaciers.

It is these three movements coming into alignment—when the Earth's orbit is at its most elliptical, the tilt is at its maximum of 24.5 degrees, and the wobble places the Earth closest to the sun during the Northern Hemisphere's summer—that initiates an interglacial.

When the Northern Hemisphere is closest to and tipped the most toward the sun during its summer, increased solar radiation reaches northern latitudes, causing accelerated rates of glacial melting. During the Northern Hemisphere's winter in this alignment the Earth is as distant from the sun as it can get and tipped maximally away from the sun, producing extremely cold winters in northern latitudes. Although you might intuitively think that cold winters would promote glaciation, the truth is just the opposite. With cold winters comes little precipitation. The combination of very dry, cold winters and radiant, warm summers causes the ice sheets and alpine glaciers in the Northern Hemisphere to wither away, initiating an interglacial. This alignment was reached eleven thousand years ago to put an end to the Wisconsin Glaciation, which had lasted one hundred thousand years.

Eighteen thousand years ago the Wisconsin's continental glaciers reached their largest size, and the Earth's average annual temperature was as cold as it had been for more than a hundred thousand years, at fifty-one degrees Fahrenheit. The large continental glacier in North America—the Laurentide Ice Sheet—covered all of Canada east of the Rocky Mountains; all of New England and New York; down through Ohio, Indiana, and Illinois into eastern Nebraska; and up through the Dakotas. Alpine glaciers in the western mountains grew and converged to cover all but the highest peaks. To produce all this ice, along with its sister ice sheet and massive complexes of alpine glaciers in Eurasia, the Earth's sea level dropped more than a hundred meters. But then the orbital cycles started to come into alignment to initiate our present interglacial, which reached its warmest period, known as the *hypsithermal*, about six thousand years ago, with a mean annual global temperature of sixty degrees. Then the Earth entered a prolonged period of global cooling—the result of the interglacial alignment moving out of synchrony.

Yet during the twentieth century we witnessed a reversal of this cooling trend, the result of human-induced global warming. At the start of the third millennium we climbed back up to a mean global temperature of sixty degrees. Most climatologists and glaciologists believe that we were primed to move into another period of glaciation at any time—that this interglacial had run its course—but it appears that global warming will hold off glaciation for possibly another thousand years or so. Even with global warming, it's most likely that ten thousand years from now many of the granite domes explored in this book will once again be encased in glacial ice. And this slow dance of repeated glaciations will continue for millions of years to come, probably until plate tectonics drive the continents from high latitudes.

It is difficult to realize that the landscapes we experience today are very atypical for the Pleistocene. As an example, for only about 5 percent of the past two million years has the Vermont landscape in which I live been dominated by forests of maple, beech, birch, pine, and hemlock. The bulk of that time it was covered by glacial ice or arctic tundra—the norm for Pleistocene New England.

This is truly a story of epic proportions. Playing on this analogy, if the Pleistocene is compared to a thousand-page novel, the part in the novel played by industrial culture—which has existed for only the past two centuries—would be represented in about two sentences. Yet look at all that has happened in those two sentences. This may be one reason why, as a culture, we have such difficulty grasping geological time.

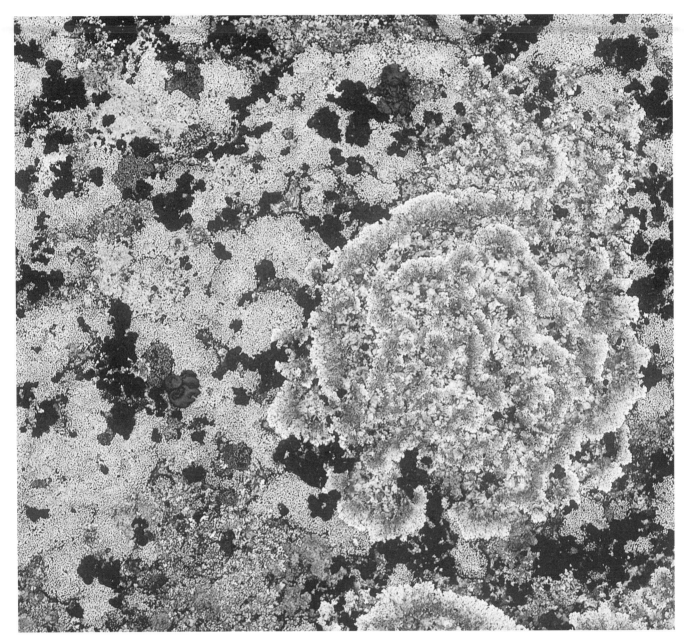

Lichen-covered granite, Acadia National Park

CHAPTER THREE

Graced with Lichen and Moss

With the onset of our current interglacial, a blanket of glacial ice was pulled away to reveal the granite domes we see today. At that time these mountains would have been striking. Glacially scoured granite bedrock would have stretched in all directions, its polished surface as glassy as the walls of city skyscrapers. With scattered glacially deposited boulders breaking the pattern, it must have been a surreal, Daliesque landscape. Although I can sense the wonder of striding over these granite surfaces, I imagine they would hold only fleeting interest compared to today's more weathered bedrock. The young, glaciated granite would have been monotonous without lichen, moss, wildflowers, or islands of contorted, windswept trees to add color, texture, and pattern. There would be no smell of pine, no sound of wind feathered by vegetation, no patchwork quilt of colorful lichen. The unrestricted views would lack the elegant frames of coniferous trees. I find today's granite mountains far more inviting—all because of rock outcrop *succession*.

Succession is one of ecology's oldest concepts, first studied and defined by Henry David Thoreau in 1856, ten years after his sojourn at Walden Pond. Although many people are familiar with Thoreau's philosophical work, few realize his important contributions to natural history and ecology. His 1859 lecture to the Middlesex Agricultural Society, "The Succession of Forest Trees," was probably the most significant.

Thoreau was interested in the process by which a forest changes over time from, say, a pine forest to one dominated by oak. He studied the dispersal of seeds, becoming the first person to note that squirrels, by caching acorns and other nuts, were important agents of forest change. He also identified wind as a significant factor in forest succession. An abandoned field on the leeward side of a pine forest would most likely succeed to another pine forest as it was colonized by windblown seeds:

> *Two or three pines will run swiftly forward a quarter of a mile into a plain, which is their favorite field of battle, taking advantage of the least shelter, as a rock, or fence, that may be there, and intrench themselves behind it, and if you look sharp, you may see their plumes waving there. Or, as I have said, they will cross a broad river without a bridge, and as swiftly climb and permanently occupy a steep hill beyond.*

Thus Thoreau not only explained changes in forest composition through time but also developed and named one of ecology's most basic concepts—succession.

Ecological succession begins when some form of physical disturbance to an ecosystem initiates a series of changes in its plant communities. Back in 1973 the land I now own was logged for its white pine, which—judging by the number of stumps—must have dominated the forest. The logging not only opened the forest to more light but also disturbed the leaf litter as the logs were dragged through the forest. This allowed black birch, a tree with very small seeds, to colonize the areas where leaf litter had been removed. The black birches are now almost a foot in diameter. American beech and sugar maple have established beneath the birch. In time it is possible that eastern hemlock will start to grow under the beech and maple. Without any future disturbance, this forest will succeed from one dominated by black birch to a forest of maple and beech, and then possibly of hemlock. All these changes in forest communities are collectively called a *sere*. Together disturbance and sere represent the process of succession.

Disturbance and the successional changes that follow it are like the opposing yet balancing yin and yang of Taoist philosophy. Both are equally important to a region's ecological well-being. When one dominates the other, a region's biodiversity will drop. If disturbance is too frequent, fragile and older ecosystems, including the species associated with them, are lost. Yet a lack of disturbance would cause a decline in those species that colonize recently altered sites. From an ecological perspective it is simply a matter of balance. On all the granite balds examined in this book the interplay between disturbance and the seral changes that follow it are continually being played out.

Thoreau initiated the study of succession, but the individual probably best known in the development of successional theory is Frederic Clements. Clements grew up in Nebraska, traveled extensively in the West, and by 1916, when he wrote his comprehensive book *Plant Succession: An Analysis of the Development of Vegetation,* was considered an authority on the vegetation of North America. He was strongly influenced by the "organismic biologists" of that time—a group of scientists who countered the increasingly mechanistic view of biological life. These biologists believed that one could not truly understand the functioning of an organism by simply examining its working components. They felt that the whole was far greater than the sum of the parts, a concept that lies at the very heart of modern systems theory.

The basic tenet of Clements's successional theory was that the process of succession eventually resulted in a mature ecosystem called the *climax.* Clements saw the climax as a kind of "superorganism" and the successional process giving rise to it as similar to the development and growth of an individual. Like the development of an organism, succession to the climax was an orderly, predictable process in which each plant community prepared the way for the next community until the stable, self-perpetuating climax was established. Just as runners in a relay race pass a baton with each lap until the race is completed, each plant community in the sere prepared the way for the next—a concept called *relay floristics.*

Clements's work had a profound impact on the field of ecology. But his dogmatic style and perceived arrogance offended a number of ecologists, who attacked his successional theory. Leading the charge was Henry Gleason, with a 1926 paper titled "The Individualistic Concept of the Plant Association." Gleason's basic premise was that communities were very loose associations of plants—just random aggregates that taken as a whole had nothing in common with an organism. Furthermore, he claimed, succession itself was a random process, highly unpredictable, showing no orderly relay floristics. As in many of the debates that have developed in ecology in the past century, there is evidence to support both Clements and Gleason.

PRIMARY AND SECONDARY SUCCESSION

Based on the nature and degree of a disturbance, ecologists have defined two basic successional patterns—*primary succession* and *secondary succession*. Primary succession follows disturbances that generate a completely *abiotic* environment—one that not only has no living organisms but also contains no soil or organic material of any kind. Volcanic activity in the form of lava flows or deep ash deposits, landslides, glaciation, and in rare cases fire followed by heavy erosion can all create primary successional sites.

Blowdowns, logging, most fires, and agricultural activity are examples of disturbances that create secondary sites, where many organisms survive the disturbance and the soil is left at least partially intact. Succession on primary sites tends to be quite Clementsian, showing relay floristics, yet succession on secondary sites is a far more random process, as Gleason described. The new plant community will be the result of numerous factors—the plants that survive the disturbance, the seeds that are already in the soil, and the seeds that invade the site following the disturbance. The interplay of these variables makes a number of successional outcomes possible on secondary sites, and predictability almost impossible. An example may help illustrate this.

A northern pine forest is logged for timber. If the harvest occurs in summer, the logs dragged through the wood will disturb the forest litter, exposing the soil. If logging happens during a winter with a deep snowpack, the leaf litter will be disturbed very little. Just this seasonal difference will have a big impact on what kind of trees will colonize the site after the logging. Many trees, such as pine, have small seeds that must germinate on exposed soil to successfully establish. Because these small seeds have limited energy storage, if they germinate on a bed of forest litter they will perish before their root takes hold. So the seasonal timing of the logging is an important variable.

The year in which the logging occurs is another critical factor. Many trees intentionally maintain low seed production for a number years in a row, storing energy that could otherwise be used to produce seeds. They then come forth with a bumper crop of seeds—as much as a hundredfold increase. These punctuated times of prolific production are called *mast years, mast* being a European term for "nut." But why would trees have developed this behavior? Why not produce seeds as the energy becomes available, rather than saving it up for some future time? Trees have developed this strategy to thwart animals that eat either their seeds or young seedlings. The low level of seed production over a few years helps set the consumers' population level. When the trees in a region have stored enough energy, they celebrate with a mast year, overwhelming their animal consumers.

The trees having a mast year at the time of logging will most likely colonize the site. Since the timing of mast years for many trees is a random occurrence, it becomes impossible to predict which trees will invade the logged pine forest. With variables such as these, it should be clear why succession following secondary disturbances is random in nature. But why then is succession on primary sites predictable?

The physical conditions plants encounter on primary sites are so extreme that only certain plants—the *pioneers*—can colonize a site following the disturbance. By growing, the pioneers slightly alter the physical conditions of the site—by stabilizing a shifting sand dune, for example—which then allows a new group of plants to take hold and gradually displace them. Each succeeding seral stage slightly moderates the physical environment, which gives access to the next seral stage—the passing of the relay floristics baton. There is perhaps no better place to observe this orderly, predictable process of primary succession than on outcroppings of glaciated granite.

SUCCESSION ON GRANITE

Consider for a moment, the harsh physical conditions that plants must contend with on a bare slab of granite. How do they get water? How do they anchor themselves? How do they secure nutrients? In combination these factors create a formidable array of conditions, so tough in fact that only one group of plants in the entire world—the *crustose lichens*—have been able to overcome them.

Actually, lichens aren't true plants. They are a close association between species of *Ascomycetes* (a major group of fungi) and either *cyanobacteria* (bacteria that photosynthesize) and/or algae. Although all the species of cyanobacteria and algae found in lichens can live on their own, the fungi depend on them to survive. The nature of this association is called *mutualism:* a relationship in which both parties benefit and that is obligatory for the survival of one or both species. Through photosynthesis the bacteria and algae produce carbohydrate energy to fuel themselves and the fungi, while the fungi grow around the bacteria or algae, creating a more hospitable environment—one that absorbs and holds nutrients and water. In this way the two or three species become one.

The next time you find yourself on a rocky outcrop, look carefully at the lichens to see which of the following four growth forms are present. The crustose lichens are morphologically the simplest. On bedrock they often look like black, gray, or green weathered paint—a thin veneer of tissue brushed directly onto the rock. *Foliose lichens,* although prostrate in their growth form, are more plantlike than crustose lichens. The wavy margins of their tissue, similar to crinkled lettuce, rise above the rock, allowing foliose lichens to capture detrital material carried over the bedrock by sheet-washed rain. The *fruiticose lichens* are structurally the most complex, sporting erect fruiting bodies that can resemble miniature goblets, trees, caribou antlers, upright snakes, and a host of other structures that would fit well in a Dr. Seuss book. Finally, *squamulose lichens* look like a hybrid of foliose and fruiticose forms. Where foliose lichens are relatively flat, squamulose lichens bulge upward like a flattened pincushion but lack any of the distinct vertical structures characteristic of fruiticose lichens. Of these four groups, it is the crustose lichens that are the first to colonize bare granite.

Crustose lichens have an array of marvelous adaptations that allow them to be the pioneers of rock outcrops. Underneath the lichen, microscopic rootlike fungal threads called *rhizinae* grow between the mineral grains of the granite, anchoring the entire lichen to the rock. To get their nutrients, crustose lichens look to the air. Many nutrients, carried into the atmosphere by wind, dissolve in rainwater, which is in turn absorbed by lichens. Many lichens having cyanobacteria can take nitrogen gas directly from the air and convert it into usable compounds such as nitrates. But possibly the most unusual adaptation found in lichens is *cryptobiosis.* Based on the Latin origins of this term, can you guess what the adaptation is?

Cryptobiosis is the ability of an organism to cease all metabolic activity and molecular reactions through complete desiccation. In other words, when lichens are in the state of cryptobiosis they might as well be dead. You could take a lichen-covered rock, place it in a vault that lacks light and humidity, and a century later remove it,

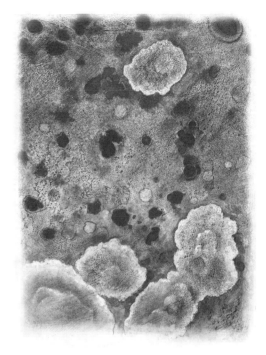

Granite covered with crustose and foliose lichens

place it in the sunlight, and spritz it with water; within a few minutes you'd see the lichens swell and begin photosynthesis and all other metabolic activities. This "on and off" habit of life allows lichens to colonize environments that can be completely desiccated for long periods of time. It is also why some lichens grow so slowly. A crustose lichen one inch in diameter, growing on an outcrop in an arid region, can be more than a hundred years old.

The first discovery of cryptobiosis occurred just after the invention of the microscope early in the seventeenth century. At that time biologists were enamored with nematodes—small, translucent, wormlike organisms—because all their organs, including their beating hearts, could be viewed through a microscope. As the story goes, a biologist, after viewing a soil nematode—one that becomes cryptobiotic when it dries out—put the glass plate holding the nematode aside. In time the nematode shriveled up and was taken for dead. But the glass plate was never washed. A few weeks or months later water was accidentally splashed on the plate. Within minutes, to the surprise of the biologist, the "dead" nematode had rehydrated and was observed crawling away. Word got out, and soil nematodes quickly became of prime interest—soon being called "resurrection worms," to the great disdain of the Catholic Church, whose protests prompted the new term *cryptobiotic worms.*

Most people are amazed when they first learn about cryptobiosis. Yet in our daily lives we are already familiar with this phenomenon. When we go to the gardening supply store and buy seeds in their tidy little packages, we are buying cryptobiotic propagules. Most seeds, particularly those of early successional plants, are cryptobiotic. Which brings to mind a puzzle I once pondered for years involving the European biennial mullein.

I knew that mullein germinated only in bare soil exposed to full sunlight. In New England forests the only sites with dense populations of this plant are in recent burns or areas that have been heavily logged. My question was this: How did so many mullein seeds, which are dispersed on the fur of mammals, manage to find these sites just after the disturbance? Were deer somehow attracted to exposed soil, possibly rolling in it and releasing mullein seeds?

Each mullein flower stalk produces tens of thousands of small black seeds about the size of fine pepper grains, which are dispersed through catapulting. An animal passing by—such as a deer—accidentally bends back the old, stiff flower stalk and then releases it. The spring action showers the deer with seeds. I now realize that mullein seeds are cryptobiotic and are randomly shed as the deer goes about its daily business. There they lie in the soil until there is a disturbance. If the disturbance opens the ground to full sunlight and the soil is exposed so that it can heat up from the sun's energy, the mullein seeds germinate. Thus the dense stands of mullein I encounter are from seeds most likely shed by many animals over a period of many years. Mullein is such a master in the realm of cryptobiosis that seeds recovered from crypts in British churches, where they had lain dormant for more than seven hundred years, came to life when planted.

With their arsenal of adaptations, crustose lichens will quickly colonize exposed granite. They accomplish this by wind-dispersed structures called *soredia*. These are microscopic balls of fungal tissue that surround a few cyanobacteria or algal cells. Once a soredium makes contact with granite, it anchors itself. It takes at least a decade of growth before crustose lichens become visible to the naked eye and close to half a century before their tissues have covered enough of the granite to allow the colonization of the next seral stage—the foliose lichens.

Foliose lichens establish and grow right on top of the crustose lichens, which they consume and kill in the process. It's rather a shock to think of a small lichen as a predator, but its predatory habit is strictly related to colonization. Once its crustose host is consumed, the foliose lichen functions much the way its predecessor did, with one exception: Since only the central regions of foliose lichens are attached to the rock, the undersides of their wavy margins capture and trap fine materials carried over the rock by wind or rain. In this way, scant though it may be, soil starts to form on the rock outcrop.

With the expansion of the foliose lichens and the development of primordial soil, the outcrop's water-holding capacity and availability of nutrients slowly increase. These changes allow the entrance of the third seral stage, the pincushion community—named for the growth form of either the squamulose lichens or pincushion mosses—which grow on top of foliose lichens and their small concentration of nutrients, again killing them in the process. The squamulose lichens are usually gray in color while the mosses are dark green, an important point for identification of these species, whose growth forms are similar and mimic the shape, in miniature, of the granite domes on which they can be found. It will take more than a century before a pincushion community appears on a granite outcrop. Of all the seral stages, this is the most fragile.

Unlike crustose and foliose lichens, species of the pincushion community don't securely anchor themselves to the rock. A few careless footsteps are all it takes to send outcrop succession back more than fifty years, because these species are easily crushed or knocked over. Since these communities are quite rare—usually found only on somewhat level granite outcrops—their protection is important. So whenever you encounter lichens or mosses that resemble dome-shaped pincushions on rock outcrops, marvel at their elegance, acknowledge that they are the elder, and give them a wide berth. Pincushion plants are the first species on the outcrop with a vertical growth form, very much like the tight pile of a carpet, which allows them to capture detrital material at rates much faster than foliose lichens can achieve. Within the body of the pincushions, soil forms to depths of many millimeters. This creates conditions conducive to the fruiticose lichens—the fourth seral stage.

Yet again the pattern is repeated as the fruiticose lichens, most often reindeer lichen, kill off the pincushions by growing on top of them. With each seral stage, water-holding capacity, nutrient availability, and soil formation increase, allowing the invasion of a new community. Eventually, dry-sited forbs and grasses displace the fruiticose lichens, and for the first time outcrop soils are stitched with roots. In time hardy shrubs, usually heaths such as low-

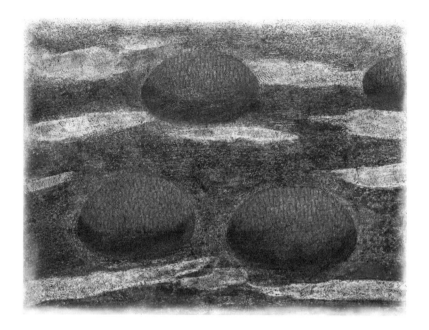

Pincushion moss on lichen-covered granite

bush blueberry or bearberry, will overtake the grasses and eventually become germination sites for dry-sited, acid-tolerant trees—either pines, spruces, or, at low elevations, oaks.

In a way it is ironic that the analogy of a relay—a team event in which all members can share victory—was used to describe this process. A more appropriate modern analogy might be a corporate acquisition, in which smaller entities are consumed by ever-larger ones. You may ask, "Why should a group of plants work to improve conditions on a rock outcrop only to allow another group to invade and eventually kill them?" It's a good question whose answer lies in a larger spatial context.

The basic strategy for all these plants is to establish, grow, and reproduce. Some plants, such as the crustose lichens, can accomplish this only in sites completely free of other plant competitors, so they have adapted to be the pioneers and take advantage of this open niche. As long as other primary sites are being created by disturbance elsewhere (here we can see the necessity of disturbance), crustose lichens will thrive in a region, even if they are eventually driven out of existence on any one particular outcrop. So the plants aren't working toward their own demise; their populations follow an ever-changing landscape mosaic generated by disturbance. On a grand scale they have found a very successful means for survival.

I mentioned earlier that pincushion communities are usually found only on granite. The attribute of granite that allows for the colonization of these plants is not related to the chemical composition of the rock but rather to its limited number of joints. In the previous chapter we saw the way expansion joints follow the curve of a granite dome, meaning that they basically run parallel to and underneath its surface. The key point is that few vertical cracks or crevices occur on granite—an important feature in the grand expanses of this bedrock. It is the absence of cracks that allows pincushion moss communities to thrive. To see how this works, we need to examine outcrop succession on bedrock with lots of vertical crevices.

While crustose lichens are starting to colonize such an outcrop, rain-washed sands start to fill the crevices, creating a new kind of primary successional site. Dry-sited species of moss, such as haircap moss (named for the fuzzy covering of its spore capsule), colonize the sand-filled crevices. The moss grows, capturing more material in its vegetation, initiating seral changes exactly like those that follow pincushion mosses—reindeer lichen, dry-sited herbs, shrubs, trees. During its successional development the crevice community expands up and out of its crevice. It then starts sprawling over the bedrock, swallowing up crustose and foliose lichens on the rock face in a fashion not unlike the sprawl of a southwestern city over the surrounding desert. Usually crevice communities merge, covering the bedrock long before pincushion plants come on the scene. Most bedrock outcrops are colonized by the expansion of crevice communities and become completely covered within a century.

Although granite often lacks crevices, it usually has scattered depressions ground by glaciers. These shallow bowls capture rain-washed sands and become colonized to form circular crevice communities. Since they are usually widely spaced and isolated on granite bedrock,

Haircap moss and reindeer lichen

these pockets give rise to vegetated islands that can last many centuries before they merge. Only on granite, or other kinds of bedrock that lack vertical crevices, does outcrop succession develop so slowly.

It is in the midst of this process on granite that outcrop succession is at its best—when the colors, textures, and patterns are the most compelling. We find a background tapestry of crustose and foliose lichen on which are placed delicate pincushions and a scattering of vegetated islands. The islands are marvels in their own right, often showing the whole seral sequence of upright-growing plants—from moss on the margins all the way to stunted trees in their centers. Supporting conifers, the islands look like many-masted schooners becalmed in a sea of granite. To me the essence of these outcrop landscapes is much like that of a desert. They are expansive, in places seemingly barren, and yet support a unique array of plants adapted to harsh conditions.

I am particularly enamored of the moss and fruiticose lichen communities on granite outcrops. Looking down at them from a few feet above, I am reminded of flying over mixed forests of conifers and hardwoods—Lilliputian woodlands surrounded by crustose-lichen-covered fields. So the next time you find yourself on exposed granite, slow your pace and acquaint yourself with these unique outcrop communities. Get down on your hands and knees and marvel at the beautiful patterns and textures of lichen and moss.

Multiple-trunked pitch pine, Acadia National Park

CHAPTER FOUR

Exposed by Fire and Ice

A number of years ago a headline in my local paper read, FIFTEEN ACRES DESTROYED BY FIRE. Interpreting it literally, it sounded as if the land itself was erased; if I visited the site, I'd stumble upon a huge gaping hole. But what I actually found was an area where about one out of every two trees had been heat-killed by the fire. I also discovered what was going to be a wonderfully productive blueberry patch in a couple of years. The acreage looked fine to me.

This headline illustrates a bias against ecological disturbance that is common within our culture. Fires, damaging winds, or floods are often seen as disasters even if they don't directly harm people, while mining and clear-cutting, which may raise concerns, are never portrayed this way. If a disturbance generates a profit or is willed by human intent, it seems, it's not a disaster. Yet natural disturbances in the landscape are critical for ecological well-being. Moderate levels of disturbance are responsible for creating rich landscape mosaics that foster a wealth of biotic diversity. Just as a person who has experienced a life completely devoid of grief and suffering might lack character and depth, a landscape untouched by disturbance would lack complexity and completeness. But in a culture that often views components of the natural world as commodities—a place to extract timber, for instance—disturbance can be an economic threat. Thus acres are "destroyed by a fire."

If it weren't for disturbance, all the exposed granite domes I explore in this book would be cloaked in forest or alpine tundra, eliminating a unique and compelling landscape. And the most widespread and common form of disturbance that has exposed our northern granite domes is fire.

Historically fire—both naturally occurring and human-caused—has played a critical role in just about all of our North American ecosystems. Desert grasslands in Arizona, jack pine forests in Michigan, the Florida Everglades, and California's magnificent stands of sequoia all owe their existence to fire. Fire has been such a common disturbance on our continent that many ecosystems have adapted fully to its presence—so fully that a lack of fire in these systems usually has very negative consequences.

I first learned this lesson when I began my graduate studies at the University of Colorado in the mid-1970s. As I started to explore the foothill forests that rose from the city of Boulder on up toward the high peaks of the Front Range, I noticed pockets of gray, standing dead ponderosa pine snags surrounded by rings of browning pines. These dying pockets were always located within the densest ponderosa stands, and there I found outbreaks of the pine bark beetle, an insect native to the region. I knew that pine bark beetles lay their eggs only under the bark of sick or dying pines. These pines don't have the energy needed to produce a copious flow of sap, which could smother and kill the pine bark beetle's eggs and subsequent larvae. But why were the insects killing large sections of the forest rather than individual unhealthy trees?

In this foothills region, where annual precipitation is less than twenty inches a year, ponderosas need ample room to grow in order to avoid intense competition for water. Historically they formed open forests with canopies that blocked less than 50 percent of the sky. I remember seeing photos taken in Boulder during the late nineteenth century, and in the background I could clearly distinguish individual pines growing on the foothills. But the forest of the 1970s was much different; it was a dense cloak of dark green where pines merged to create closed forest canopies. In these crowded forests the ponderosa pines were dramatically weakened by competition, to the extent that they couldn't protect themselves from the pine bark beetle, allowing this native insect to explode to epidemic proportions.

The difference was the result of fire suppression. These forests had evolved with fire for thousands of years, which the ponderosa pines came to rely on to thin their stands so they could thrive. A major agent of fire in the foothills of Colorado were its Native inhabitants.

Native Americans throughout the present United States used fire as an important management tool, creating ecosystems that were more productive in berries, nuts, and wildlife. In my home region of New England, Native peoples used fire to create woodlands with open understories that were free of forest litter; there game could be quietly stalked and more easily seen at close range, to be killed with bow and arrow. Today New England's forests have dense understories in which successful use of bow and arrow while stalking game is almost impossible. Another result of burning these forests was that they became much more productive in generating food for both humans and wildlife. Fire selected for thick-barked, nut-bearing trees such as oaks, chestnuts, and hickories. Where fires thinned understory vegetation, ample light reached the ground, and fire-tolerant stands of blueberries and huckleberries thrived.

Burning in the foothill forests of Colorado also enhanced wildlife habitat and generated increased berry production. And as mentioned previously, over thousands of years of burning the forest ecosystem adapted to the presence of fire. When settlers arrived in the nineteenth century, not only did they *not* continue the practice of burning the forest, but they engaged in fire suppression as well, unwittingly creating conditions that years later would threaten the entire forest.

Fire suppression in other ecosystems has created different problems. In the Everglades it resulted in the loss of small, open bodies of water. During periods of drought, fire in the

Glades can burn deep into peat deposits, which later fill with water to create a mosaic of impoundments—critical habitat for many wading birds and alligators. Fire suppression in stands of California's giant sequoia allowed white fir and incense cedar to invade the understory. When a fire did occur, these smaller trees could potentially carry the flames into the crowns of the huge trees, which historically had been immune to the impacts of fire. The lack of fire also curtailed sequoia regeneration, since the trees' small seeds establish only on bare soil created through the removal of forest litter. Fire suppression in Michigan negatively affected jack pine forests and almost caused the demise of the Kirtland's warbler, which depends on jack pine for nesting habitat. Overgrazing and associated suppression of fire have almost completely converted Arizona's rich, high-desert grasslands into mesquite-filled thickets.

Fire is an important part of this country's natural heritage, and we are slowly realizing that it needs to be a component of our management plans. Today just about every national park either has "let-go" areas where wildfires are allowed to burn, or uses "controlled burns" to maintain ecosystems that would otherwise be lost.

FIRE AND GRANITE

Granite balds and fire have a relationship that is just about as tightly coupled as a beach and its waves. What is it about granite that creates such fire-prone ecosystems? One important feature is its limited number of vertical joints, which means that almost all precipitation flows over and off the bedrock; very little of it infiltrates. Second, due to its granular texture, granite weathers into thin, coarse, extremely well-drained, acidic substrates that often have the consistency of Grape-Nuts cereal. Combined, these attributes make granite a drier environment than any other kind found in northern regions. Due to its highly acidic substrate, only certain species of woody plants can colonize and grow on granite. Most notable are members of the heath family (blueberry, huckleberry, bearberry, manzanita) and members of the yellow pine group (lodgepole, jack, and pitch pines). All these species thrive in dry, acidic, nutrient-poor sites; all produce vegetation and litter that is highly flammable; and all are strongly adapted to fire.

The heaths reproduce not only sexually through the production of berries but also asexually through *rhizomes* (stems that run just under the soil and can sprout new aboveground plants), creating extensive clones. Unlike the rhizomes of many species of plants, those of fire-adapted heaths can tolerate extremely high temperatures, so fires remove competitors and allow these heaths to grow more vigorously. Repeated fires thicken stands of heaths, which produce more fuel for future fires, creating a positive-feedback loop. In such a regime heaths come to carpet the ground.

Lodgepole, jack, and pitch pines also have an interesting array of adaptations to fire. The most obvious is that all three species have developed cone serotiny. *Serotinous cones* do not open when they mature at two years of age (as most other pines), but stay welded shut by a surface coating of heavy resin. Inside these cones pine seeds remain viable for up to twenty-five years. Serotinous cones will open only when heat melts the resin. Most of the research in this area has been done by William Beaufait on jack pine, which produces more serotinous cones per unit of biomass than any other species of pine on this continent.

Jack pine cones that are serotinous will not open until they are heated above 120 degrees Fahrenheit. At 140 degrees they open to shed their seeds in twelve hours; at 200 degrees the cones open in one and a half minutes. Thus the timing of cone opening is directly related to the amount of heat produced by a fire, a marvelous adaptation in these species whose small seeds need to land on bare soil to successfully establish. In cooler ground fires the seeds are often released after the fire is out. In hot crown fires, however, the seeds are released into the blaze—a strategy that at first doesn't seem to make sense. But jack pine seeds can withstand a temperature of seven hundred degrees for fifteen seconds, enough time to make it to the ground (ideally landing in an area that's not actively burning) or to be carried away by a strong updraft, potentially colonizing a site miles away. Since a jack pine can produce

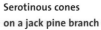

tens of thousands of seeds, many will survive even the hottest fires. Cone serotiny is a highly evolved trait and gives these species of pine a head start in colonizing sites disturbed by fire.

The frequency of fire in a region can sometimes be determined by the percentage of serotinous cones on members of these fire-adapted species. In areas where fires historically come every few decades, most cones will display serotiny, since trees with a lot of serotinous cones leave more offspring following a fire. But in areas where the frequency of fire is measured in centuries, few if any cones will be serotinous, because seeds within those cones are viable only for about twenty-five years. Here the trees with serotinous cones will produce few offspring; those with regular cones that open when they mature at two years have the better reproductive strategy.

To find serotinous cones on jack, lodgepole, or pitch pine, look for tightly shut cones that lie three or more twig whorls back from the tip of any branch. Regular cones this far back will have already matured and opened, since pines produce one whorl of twigs each year. A cone three twig whorls down a branch is three years old. Those farther down are even older.

All three species also produce highly flammable bark, foliage, and litter that encourages fire. Only through frequent fire can these species hold dominance in areas where they grow. Without fire, other species of tree that can grow more vigorously will outgrow and kill off these pines. Like the heaths, they need fire to keep competitors at bay.

Of the three species, pitch pine has the greatest array of fire adaptations. Lodgepole and jack pines do best in areas where frequent hot fires are the norm, and they mostly rely on their serotinous cones to keep them present in high numbers. Because their thin bark is very flammable they are usually killed by these fires. But pitch pine relies less on serotiny and more on resisting direct damage from fire. Unlike lodgepole and jack pine, pitch pine has extremely thick bark that protects its cambial tissues from being damaged by heat. In this way many pitch pines survive hot blazes. Second, the trunks of pitch pine are covered in tufts of needles that at their base, deep within the bark, hold *adventitious buds*. If the cambial tissue at a certain height of the trunk is killed, girdling the tree, the area directly below it will sprout new branches from its adventitious buds. Even a tree girdled at ground level will stump-sprout, something neither a lodgepole nor a jack pine can do.

A stump-sprouted, multiple-trunked pitch pine

SNOW AND ICE

On a number of the higher domes in the West — those at elevations of more than ten thousand feet — fire plays less of a role. Instead ice and snow become the agents that keep granite exposed.

As snow piles up on the ground, the bottom of the snowpack metamorphoses into *firn* — icy granules that have lost the crystalline pattern of snowflakes. Through compaction or seepage of water under the snowpack, the firn turns into ice. When the snowpack warms up on granite slopes, water from the melting snow flows under the ice, lubricating the granite. The integrated snowpack then slides down the bedrock, resulting in what is called *ice creep*, scraping off anything attached to the granite other than crustose lichens or free-living cyanobacteria. In this way steep granite slabs are perennially kept free of almost all vegetation. This was clearly visible on the first dome I climbed in Yosemite.

Driving into the park from the west on Route 120, the very first dome I encountered was Lembert. I met my friends Chris Papouchis and Andrew Stemple in the parking lot adjacent to this dome, and within five minutes they were dragging me up Lembert's south face, which at times had a pitch close to forty-five degrees. Ice creep on this dome has kept the granite clean and white, with only a scattering of gray crustose lichen.

On other high domes with gentler relief, winter snow loads can build up to such depths that they don't melt out until late summer, creating growing seasons that are simply too short for plants — in some cases even for crustose lichens. This condition is most apparent in the North Cascades, where snow piles up to impressive depths. There the wind-exposed sides of granite outcrops become covered with funaria, a cryptobiotic moss that looks and feels like black velvet. But on the adjacent leeward side, where snowdrifts cover the granite well into summer, nothing grows on the rock. Even depressions that should support crevice communities hold only unvegetated, exposed sands.

Finally, on the highest domes I visited, those higher than eleven thousand feet in the Wind Rivers, wind is also a factor in keeping granite exposed. On the tops of these domes the rock is carpeted with crustose lichens, but strong winter winds blast off foliose and other forms of lichen, holding succession at bay. Crevice communities develop extremely slowly due to the combination of short growing seasons and winds that keep them tucked within the bedrock.

The nature of granite, together with the geological forces that have sculpted it over time, the plants that colonize its unyielding surface, and the disturbances that counter their successional development, create a granite bald. So consistent are these processes that granite domes across the country share many similarities. Yet the granite mountains of each region of the United States hold their own distinctiveness. Each has its particular attraction, and each is worthy of extensive exploration. The following chapters highlight the special qualities that can be experienced within each mountainous region of the country that is graced by glacially scoured granite.

PART TWO

AMERICA'S GRANITE MOUNTAINS

Looking north from the south ridge of Cadillac Mountain, Acadia National Park

CHAPTER FIVE

Acadia: Land of Fire and Fog

As above, so below. This aphorism came out of Christian mysticism during the first millennium, but I'd guess that its roots are far older. All around us patterns are repeated at many different spatial scales, as I'm sure ancient peoples around the globe were well aware tens of thousands of years ago. The spiral of a galaxy is reflected in a hurricane, a whirlpool of water, and the arrangement of scales on a pinecone. But only recently, with the development of chaos theory and fractal geometry, has the study of this phenomenon been incorporated into the realm of science.

Fractals are patterns that repeat. Take a head of broccoli; at each fork its florets are structured exactly like the entire head. Feathers, clouds, fern fronds, snowflakes, and watersheds are all fractals—their patterns repeat as we examine ever-smaller parts of their structure. As above, so below.

As I sit atop Bald Peak in Maine's Acadia National Park, I am struck by the fractal nature of this glaciated landscape. To my left lies a glacial notch that separates Norumbega Mountain from the ridge systems where I sit. This deep U-shaped trough is one of seven that dissect the ridges of Mount Desert Island—the heart of this national park. During my hike to Bald Peak from the notch I crossed a series of smaller U-shaped cuts ten to thirty feet deep where the bedrock had been glacially quarried. In front of me, at a still-smaller scale but in the same pattern, lies a graceful U-shaped glacial groove about three feet across, and next to it a steep-walled U-shaped crevice only three inches deep. All these glacial gouges trace a straight line tipped just slightly west of north — the path of the Laurentide Ice Sheet.

Although only about forty thousand acres — tiny in the realm of national parks — Acadia is the country's fourth most visited park, only a little less popular than Yosemite, Yellowstone, and the Grand Canyon. It may be the mountains that rise directly out of Penobscot Bay, or the dramatic wave-pounded rocky coast, or the extensive system of carriage roads that attracts most visitors, but for me it's the exposed, fractal nature of the island's glaciated granite.

In my opinion Mount Desert Island offers the finest landscape to be found in the north-eastern United States. I know of no other area where so many different forest and outcrop communities are woven so tightly together. On my descent from Bald Peak via Parkman Mountain during this fall afternoon, I walk through expanses of open granite ledges. I step into red-and-purple patchworks of heaths. I drop abruptly into steep-walled pockets of yellow birch forest with striped maple understories, and later others housing stands of red spruce and white pine. I clamber up onto Japanese-garden-like arrangements of clumps of northern white cedar. I encounter all these very different communities, not just once but many times, within the span of half a mile. Nowhere else have I experienced a landscape with so many different textures in such a small area.

Time slows down as I wander the granite balds of this island. I'm reminded of Einstein's theory of relativity — that our perception of time is inversely related to the speed at which we travel. Only here the variable is not my hiking speed but rather the accelerated rate of new perceptions I'm picking up from all these community changes. As we age, the frequency of encountering new experiences slows, and as a result time for us accelerates. As young children summers seemed to last for years, because they were filled with all sorts of new impressions. Now, as adults, summers are shorter, and they will continue to shorten as we age and have fewer opportunities to experience new things. Yet if we travel to a different part of the world, with unusual landscapes and cultures, our experience of time again slows down as the rate of new perceptions increases. That time is relative is not just an abstract theory; it is an intrinsic aspect of our experience of life. And here I encounter it on Mount Desert Island.

I stop my descent to rest. With the sun low in the west, I can catch the sheen reflected from the glacial polish that surrounds me. Patches of polish the size of a nickel cover about 30 percent of this granite. It is a testament to the rock's ability to resist weathering that only about a quarter of an inch has eroded down from its original polished surface in the past thirteen thousand years. Yet thirteen thousand years is a mere snippet of time to this island's granite, which was formed more than 360 million years ago during the Acadian Orogeny.

ACADIA'S BIRTH

At that time a small, wandering crustal plate called Avalonia came into contact with what is now New England and shortly thereafter got crunched in a major collision between northern Europe and North America. The collision resulted in the subduction of portions of Avalonia deep enough to completely melt it. As the magma cooled, at depths many miles below the Earth's surface, the granites of Mount Desert Island formed. I use the plural form of *granite* because three different types occur on this island. The pink, coarse-grained, Cadillac Mountain granite is the most extensive, dominating the island east of Somes Sound. To the west of the sound lies the pink, medium-grained Somesville granite, and south of it the light gray, fine-grained Southwest Harbor granite.

A span of 360 million years is hard to comprehend. Even thirteen thousand years is difficult to fathom, since our personal experience of large units of time is usually measured in decades. To help grasp the immensity of time represented by these granites, let's develop an analogy. Suppose that the thickness of one page in this book represents one century. A stack of a thousand pages, roughly five inches high, would represent one hundred thousand years, about the tenure of our species—modern *Homo sapiens*—on this planet. How high would the stack need to be to represent 360 million years? It would be roughly the height of Cadillac Mountain — Acadia's highest summit — fifteen hundred feet high, a stack of paper 50 percent taller than the Empire State Building. Now, that's a lot of centuries!

Through this period of time miles of overlying metamorphic rock, thrust up into a major mountain range by the Acadian Orogeny, slowly eroded away to expose the granites of Mount Desert Island. Then during the Pleistocene glaciations of the past two million years, wave after wave of glacial ice sculpted the island's granite into its present series of exposed north–south ridges and glacial notches. With the retreat of the Laurentide Ice Sheet thirteen thousand years ago, many of the notches filled with water to form either lakes, or, in the case of the ocean-flooded Somes Sound, the only fjord in the eastern United States other than the lower Hudson River.

Evidence of the last glaciation is ever apparent on Acadia's exposed ridges. Rounded glacial boulders dot the landscape, the most famous of which is Bubble Rock just north of Jordan Pond. Having a diameter of more than ten feet and balanced on the open, steep slab of South Bubble Mountain, this boulder provides good material for the imagination. Glacial polish and grooves are ubiquitous on Mount Desert's granite, but glacial striations are difficult to find on its hard surface. Instead, boulders embedded in the bottom of the glacial ice and dragged over the bedrock were at times driven into the granite by slow but powerful internal movements of the ice, chipping out chatter marks. Large chatter marks on slabs sloping to the south often capture coarse sands eroded from the granite and house crevice communities.

Each exposed ridge on Mount Desert displays numerous elegantly sculpted whalebacks, and, on an even larger scale, roche moutonnées with their steep southern faces quarried into cliffs by the passing glacial ice — the Beehive near Sand Beach being the most obvious example. All these features, both large and small, have remained exposed on Acadia's ridgetops since the retreat of the Laurentide Ice Sheet.

Although he never set foot on the island, Samuel de Champlain—the first European to describe it—noted the island's barren nature. He served as pilot and guide to Sieur de Monts, who had received a grant from Henry IV for La Cadie (Acadia). The grant comprised all of North America from forty to forty-six degrees latitude—basically from Philadelphia to Montreal.

De Monts established his first colony in 1604 on an island near the mouth of the St. Croix River, which now separates Maine from New Brunswick. In September of that year he sent Champlain out to explore the coast of his new domain. Rounding Schoodic Point and attracted by smoke from an Abenaki encampment near the Otter Cliffs, Champlain had his first view of the island. He wrote, "This island is very high, and cleft into seven or eight mountains, all in a line. The summits of most of them are bare of trees, nothing but rock. I named it l'Isle des Monts-deserts" (the isle of bare mountains).

To the eastern Abenaki who summered on Pemetic (their name for this island of "mountain ranges"), *barren* or *bare* probably didn't match their experience. Pemetic was bountiful. Its granite bedrock brought forth a cornucopia of blueberries and huckleberries, which were gathered and dried. Its mudflats and rocky shores yielded clams and mussels that were also dried on lines made from the roots of spruce trees. And its waters offered fish and seals whose flesh was smoked and preserved.

The Abenaki spent summers gathering and preparing this bounty for winter, but also feasting on all that the island had to offer. When the leaves turned in October, they filled birch-bark canoes with preserved foods and made their way back up Maine's major rivers to their winter village encampments, safe from harsh coastal storms. For millennia before Champlain ever laid eyes on Mount Desert, the island sustained eastern Abenaki tribes; today it remains a haven for millions of visitors. Barren it was to Champlain, but bountiful it has been to so many.

Granite, and the fire regime it supports, creates the drama in Acadia. Although he didn't know it, what Champlain saw were mountain ridges kept bare by fire. The frequency of fire has molded the ecosystems of this landscape, but *frequency* is a relative term. On Acadia's granite, growth is exceedingly slow. Summer fog banks frequently well up from Penobscot Bay to cloak the island—reducing photosynthetic rates—and winter nor'easters and north-western gales rake the ridgetops. One summit fire every few hundred years is enough to keep these mountains perpetually exposed.

The most recent fire to affect Mount Desert occurred in mid-October 1947. Starting in a dump west of Hulls Cove, the fire consumed more than seventeen thousand acres in ten days—most of it in a triangle between Bar Harbor, Eagle Lake, and Otter Cliffs. The imprint of this fire is visible in the young aspen and birch forests that sprouted in its aftermath, as well as the numerous dead pine snags felled near hiking trails in this area of the park. I first heard about the 1947 fire as an undergraduate in a wildlife management class at the University of New Hampshire. But it wasn't until I returned from my graduate studies in Colorado that I saw for myself the evidence of this fire.

My wife Marcia, daughter Kelsey, and I were ambling along the south ridge of Champlain Mountain through glorious groves of pitch pine—a natural landscape that could have inspired the design of a Japanese tea garden. These pitch pines, sculpted by the severe winds of winter nor'easters, resembled large bonsai trees that framed passageways from one granite-floored, meditative space to another. As we slowly descended, surrounded by the blue of the ocean with Maine's islands spread out before us, I suddenly noticed that the pitch pines were gone. They were quickly replaced by a thicket of aspen, and then I saw the downed trunks of white pine and their severed stumps. This was visible evidence of the '47 fire.

For the next mile, until we reached the park loop road near Sand Beach, the evidence of fire was everywhere. As a budding "reader of the landscape," I couldn't contain myself in pointing

Open grove of pitch pine on Champlain Mountain

out basal fire scars, multiple-trunked red maple, and thickets of young birch and aspen. And then to the southwest of the Beehive we entered a beautiful young grove of pure paper birch. Before I could utter a word about the need for birch seeds to land in bare soil to successfully establish, Marcia said, "Let's just appreciate this magnificent birch forest for what it is." We stopped walking, I stopped talking, and for a number of moments we relished the beauty of this forest. Although there is a general bias in American culture against wildfire, during our time in that birch forest its workings were worshiped.

The '47 fire consumed the forests that surrounded Cadillac, Dorr, Champlain, and Gorham Mountains as well as a substantial portion of their ridgetop pitch pine communities. But fires often miss sections of forest. Although exceedingly dry and windy conditions existed at the time of the '47 fire, there may not have been enough fuel to carry the fire throughout the tops of Mount Desert's eastern ridges. Some fire-generated pitch pine groves on this section of the island predate the fire. Pitch pines on the southern ridge of Cadillac reach basal diameters of more than twenty inches, suggesting that they are well over a century in age.

That pitch pines only a foot in diameter could be a hundred years old is striking, but in fact many of these trees are older still. Pitch pine is the only conifer in the northeastern portion of the continent that can stump-sprout after being cut or heat-killed by a fire. Pines that stump-sprout develop two or three trunks that originate from one root system. So any multiple-trunked specimens with trunks more than a foot in diameter were almost certainly forced to stump-sprout from a fire more than a century earlier. Multiple-trunked specimens of this species can have root systems more than three hundred years old.

Because fires are infrequent on Mount Desert's balds, the pitch pines in Acadia lack serotinous cones. Some tightly closed cones, more than three twig whorls back from branch tips, can be found on the island's pitch pine, but these are infertile cones and, if opened, lack seeds. Yet cone serotiny does exist in Mount Desert's other fire-adapted conifer, the jack pine.

Three-toothed cinquefoil

Mount Desert Island is the only place in New England where the ranges of these two pines overlap, and a good place to see these species side by side is on the southern ridge of Cadillac Mountain.

FREQUENT FOG

The southern ridge of Champlain Mountain is one of my favorite Acadian haunts. This eastern ridge supports one of the most elegant open stands of pitch pine I have ever encountered. Today I'm seated on a sloping slab of granite, framed by pitch pines that invaded crevices long since buried under the carpet of heaths that now ring this meditative space. I'm also bathed in one of Mount Desert's familiar fogs.

On days of dense fog, the colors of lichen and moss on Acadia's balds become almost iridescent. I wandered just a hundred meters off Champlain's cairn-marked trail to this spot, one

Target lichen

of thousands that I could choose on these fog-draped ridges—perfect places to stop, sit, and reflect. The fog naturally induces me to turn my gaze toward my immediate surroundings.

Five feet in front of me is a small crevice community packed with three-toothed cinquefoil (pronounced SINK-foil). Its lustrous deep green leaves end in three small serrations, each holding a perfect sphere of condensed fog. This is an alpine plant—a common resident of heath communities found above tree line on the Northeast's highest peaks. Here I find it growing almost one mile lower in elevation than its natural habitat. Sometimes associated with the three-toothed cinquefoil on Mount Desert Island are two other alpine plants—mountain cranberry and black crowberry—but these rarer residents are absent from this crevice. The presence of these three species suggests harsh alpinelike conditions on Acadia's low-elevation balds. Strong winter winds are one factor giving rise to these conditions; summer fog is another.

On the far side of the cinquefoil crevice the granite is a mosaic of color. Splotches that look like various shades of smooth gray paint are three different species of lecanora. Associated with them is Mount Desert's other common crustose lichen, the iridescent, black-studded green map lichen. Atop the crustose lichens grow two species of rock tripe, a small black variety and a larger, warty gray species. Along with the rock tripe is another intriguing foliose lichen, the pale green target lichen—named for its ability to grow in concentric rings. The pink color is the granite itself, cleaned of its crustose lichens by the outwardly migrating rings of the target lichen. In my experience no other granite in the entire United States is carpeted with such a luxuriant growth of vibrantly colored lichens—the reason being that no other mountains experience Acadia's frequent fogs, condensed by the cold water of Penobscot Bay.

But it's not just on Mount Desert's balds that fog creates its magic—its forests and their extensive *cryptogamic carpets* are also products of its workings. *Cryptogam* is Latin for "hidden seed," meaning that these vegetative carpets are composed of spore producers such as mosses and lichens. Wherever older conifer forests—red spruce and white pine—have developed and covered Mount Desert's granite, their floors become graced with extensive mats of mosses and fruiticose lichens. *Polytrichum, Sphagnum,* and *Cladina* represent the major genera that dominate these Lilliputian realms, but close observation of the number of species present in Acadia's cryptogamic carpets reveals an astounding level of diversity. I can't quite explain why these mats of moss and lichen are so compelling to me. Maybe it's their ability to mimic the structure of the forest overstory, or the texture they add to the understory? I can only say that I find extraordinary elegance in these carpeted forests.

Where the island's forests have developed on glacial till rather than granite bedrock, they are dominated by hardwoods such as maple, beech, birch, and ash. Although the leaf litter of these trees restricts the development of cryptogamic carpets by smothering them, older stands often support an amazing array of mosses and lichens in the form of *epiphytes* (plants that grow on trees), which festoon the trunks of maple and ash. Probably the most impressive of these epi-

Lungwort

phytes is the foliose lichen lungwort, named for its resemblance to the internal structure of a lung. This bold green lichen is rare in New England forests, found almost exclusively in old-growth sections where humidity levels are relatively high. But on Mount Desert Island lungwort is common. Whether you're strolling through Acadia's conifer or hardwood forests, the fog-fed, opulent growth of moss and lichen creates a magical experience.

If you want to witness Mount Desert's forests in their full glory, head just west of Black Woods Campground to Hunters Brook. This watershed was spared by the 1947 fire and supports one of the most intriguing older forests on the island. It's composed of a mixture of large hemlock, red spruce, white pine, yellow birch, white ash, and red maple, with cryptogams carpeting the areas dominated by conifers and epiphytes cloaking the trunks of hardwoods. This diverse mixture of trees is created by the variety of soils that Hunters Brook traverses, including clays laid down during the retreat of the Laurentide Ice Sheet (these being visible in the brook's channel and cut banks). A walk along the brook offers a peaceful, almost cathedral-like experience. Yet, as is so characteristic of the island's dramatic changes, this lush watershed forest lies less than half a mile from Cadillac's exposed granite ridge, which like all of Acadia's balds hosts an anomalous species of tree.

Northern white cedar is common to rich swamps or moist upland sites in northern portions of New England, almost the antithesis of Acadia's nutrient-poor, dry granite. But on Mount Desert Island northern white cedar rivals pitch pine and red spruce in the colonization of crevice communities. Although I have never seen research on the peculiar presence of this species on Mount Desert's balds, I hypothesize that fog is primarily responsible for its establishment in such an unlikely site.

The foliage of northern white cedar is composed of small overlapping needles that create wide, flat splays of green. These splays trap and condense an incredible amount of water from fog. I know from direct experience while hiking Mount Desert's ridges on cloud-capped days that one accidental brush against a northern white cedar is a soaking encounter, certainly far more so than a brush against red spruce or pitch pine. Northern white cedar literally drip with fog, whose droplets fall into the crevice that supports their roots. In this way coastal fogs not only give the crevices greater moisture than we might imagine but also contribute dissolved nutrients such as calcium (which is carried into the air by the ocean spray), enriching the substrate of the crevice community. Whether or not this hypothesis is correct, the unusual presence of northern white cedar is most appreciated by Mount Desert's deer.

Deer prefer this species for its browse. All the outcrop cedars on Acadia's balds are misshapen and many-branched as a result of heavy, repeated browsings. From a distance, stands of northern white cedar look as if crews of landscapers had been hired to shear all branches five feet above ground level to expose their graceful trunks. The first time I noticed this phenomenon was just after descending Pemetic Mountain to Bubble Pond. As I admired the reflection of Cadillac's exposed ledges in the pond's deep, still water, I saw a gently rounded ledge colonized by cedars whose browsed lower branches perfectly mimicked the curve of the ledge. Once observed, northern white cedar's uniform browse lines stand in stark contrast to the more irregular appearance of pine or spruce.

Glaciated granite, fire, fog, and winter gales define Mount Desert Island. Because its mountains rise out of the sea and are backed by a relatively level landscape to the north, Acadia's ridges are exposed to harsh winds from frigid Alberta clippers out of the northwest and intense winter nor'easters—powerful cyclonic storms common to this section of the Gulf of Maine. We need only examine the unvegetated zone that rises above Mount Desert's ocean-facing coastline to see the impact of nor'easters. Great Head, Otter Cliffs, and the sea cliffs below Black Woods Campground are all free of vegetation for close to six stories above the high-tide mark—all from waves generated by powerful nor'easters. What must it be like to have thirty-foot waves breaking on these headlands? Having seen pictures of nor'easter-driven waves crashing over thirty-foot lighthouses, I can only imagine.

It's not just on the coast that these gales have left their mark—Acadia's exposed ridges display their work, too. Pitch pine, red spruce, and white cedar bend and twist toward the west on east-facing exposures (from nor'easter winds) and toward the southeast on west-facing exposures (from northwest gales). Stripped of needles and twigs by the ice-blasting of strong winter winds, trees growing on Mount Desert's ridges have to contend with not only establishing themselves on granite and incessant fog but loss of limb as well—all dramatically slowing their rate of growth. But the slow growth of these outcrop trees and their associated inability to form closed canopies allow for the vigorous growth of the understory heaths. Low-bush blueberry, black huckleberry, sheep laurel, and the common nonheath associate black chokeberry carpet the granite from which tree islands emerge.

The heaths and chokeberry thrive on granite; growing prostrate to it, they are protected by snow cover from the ravaging winds of winter. There is no better time to appreciate these communities (unless you want to forage for their berries) than early October, when the heaths turn a rich wine red and the chokeberry flames crimson. Draped over the tapestry of outcrop lichen and disrupted by pockets of conifer green, Acadia's heath mats are a feast for the eyes.

As I sit atop Pemetic Peak, surrounded by lichen-encrusted granite and a purple-and-red patchwork of heath, I am awed by the way the combined impacts of glaciers, winter winds, fire, and fog have generated such astounding variety in this granitic landscape. You might think that with so many strong forces at work, these domes would lie barren. But of all the balds I have visited, Acadia's are by far the most diverse and varied.

Looking south from the summit of Noonmark Mountain in the Adirondacks

CHAPTER SIX

The Whites and Adirondacks: Fragile Summits

Unlike the other mountainous regions covered in this book, the granite domes of the Northeast's interior mountains are scattered here and there, never creating extensive ranges of glaciated granite. Although exposed granite bedrock—the surface of batholiths that underlie the White Mountains of New Hampshire and the Adirondacks of New York—is common, it's most frequently seen in glaciated valley walls as cliff faces or exposed slides (like those seen on the mountain's slope in the preceding photograph). Most of the region's summits remain capped by metamorphic rock, making the few granite balds islands in a sea of forested peaks. These scattered domes also share another feature that distinguishes them from all other northern granite balds—they tend to be more heavily vegetated. At elevations of three to four thousand feet fire is rare, windblown snows don't accumulate to produce late-lying snowbanks, and ice creep is restricted to the steepest topography, so lush vegetated carpets cover much of the granite.

These eastern domes are graced by extensive mats of haircap moss, reindeer lichen, low-bush blueberry, and a mixture of other alpine heaths such as mountain cranberry, Labrador tea, and bog bilberry, plus black crowberry (a strong associate that isn't a heath). After rain, when these plants are bejeweled with droplets that resemble semiprecious stones and their grays and various shades of greens are almost fluorescent, I become a captive of their beauty. There is no doubt that these ample alpine beds are the draw of these mountainous domes. But hiking pressure is taking its toll on these unique summits. It is becoming difficult to find pristine domes with intact vegetation.

I first became aware of this when Nat Scrimshaw, a friend and colleague from my days as a teacher at the Putney School (an independent secondary school in Putney, Vermont), asked me to serve as ecological adviser for a new not-for-profit organization he had founded—the Sandwich Range Conservation Association (SRCA).

The Scrimshaws had old roots in Waterville Valley, New Hampshire, as one of the first families to settle there in the nineteenth century. Nat had grown up hiking the mountains that framed the valley and developed a strong interest in their protection through wise stewardship. Founding the SRCA was Nat's attempt to protect heavily used areas within the Sandwich Range Wilderness and adjacent peaks. In partnership with the White Mountain National Forest, the SRCA developed restoration, monitoring, and hiker education projects. So it was that I found myself as an adviser to a restoration project on Mount Welch—a beautiful granite dome four miles southwest of Waterville Valley.

At less than three thousand feet in elevation, Mount Welch and its sister summit, Dickey, never came to my attention during my college days as a member of the New Hampshire Outing Club. And I wasn't the only one unaware of these exquisite mountains. Still, even though hiker traffic was much higher on many of the White Mountains' taller peaks, parts of Mount Welch had been areas heavily impacted by footfall.

Hikers beginning an ascent of Mount Welch will find themselves going up a gentle trail through a forest dominated by sugar maple and beech, which soon gives way to one dominated by red spruce—an indication that the underlying substrate has changed to granite. In a short distance the red spruce forest opens onto a glorious granite ledge with lush islands of outcrop communities dominated by haircap moss, billowing bundles of green-and-gray reindeer lichen, and extensive mats of low-bush blueberry. Actually, the lush islands are restricted to the portion of the ledge above the trail, which soon loses its distinct path. Two hundred feet farther ahead the exposed granite ledge ends in an abrupt cliff, giving powerful, precipitous views of the valley and surrounding mountains. When hikers reach the beginning of the ledge, they head directly to the view, trampling any interceding vegetation.

On my first visit to this ledge it was obvious that the outcrop communities had been heavily degraded. Originally about half of the gently sloping, smooth granite had been covered with islands of moss, lichen, and blueberry, creating a wonderful mosaic with the crustose-lichen-covered granite. This was easily discerned by the large amount of the bedrock that was free of crustose lichens—areas once covered by outcrop communities that had completely eroded away. Coarse sand, with the consistency of Grape-Nuts cereal (the substrate that underlay the eroded outcrop islands) lay exposed throughout the ledge. Mount Welch had been known for over a century as the best blueberry-picking spot in the region. Now people needed to venture well off the trail to find blueberries.

In his efforts toward the recovery of Mount Welch's granite ledges, Nat hired Dick Fortin as a weekend summit steward to help educate hikers about protecting the fragile vegetation and to figure out a way to keep hikers on a prescribed trail. To accomplish this, Dick decided to ask hikers to ferry a rock or two up to the ledge. His intent was to delineate a trail with rocks on both sides to keep people from wandering across the outcrop communities. Soon he had a large pile of stones on the ledge, with a plan to start marking the trail the following weekend. But Dick was greeted with a real surprise the next Saturday when he reached the ledge—his pile was gone. The rocks had been used to tightly surround each remaining outcrop island, making the ledge look more like a tidy Japanese tea garden than a wilderness mountain. Dick later found out that during the preceding week a woman and her grandson had seen the rock pile, noted the impacted vegetation, and literally taken matters into their own hands. Surrounding each outcrop island with stones was their way to protect them.

Mount Welch's rock-rimmed outcrop communities

That weekend Dick noticed something unusual. Up until this point every effort he had made to block hikers from traversing outcrop vegetation, other than directly stopping them and asking them to skirt around it, had failed. He had even witnessed hikers crashing through piles of dead branches that he'd placed to block their route to the view spot. But that week-end not one person stepped within a stone ring. Somehow the rings did something no other method had accomplished. They made the delineation of a trail unnecessary and actually were probably even more effective. I have seen many hikers in White Mountains' alpine zones disregard trails lined by stones, but no one disregards the stone rings. It may be that people chafe at having their access restricted by a delineated trail in an open landscape, but are far more agreeable to the idea that they can roam freely except in specified areas.

The rings also provided another benefit: They stabilized the erosion of the sandy substrate on the sloping granite, which has subsequently begun to recolonize with haircap moss and reindeer lichen. When White Mountain National Forest personnel found out about the stone rings, they decided they needed to be removed, since they were out of place in this moun-tain setting. The problem for the forest service was that the rings were beneficial to restora-tion and revegetation of the heavily impacted ledge. In order to remove the rings, the forest service would need to be involved in a National Environmental Policy Act (NEPA) review to show that the removal would not have negative environmental consequences. The forest service decided not to become engaged in NEPA, and the stone rings remain to this day.

This is an amazing story of serendipity—one of my very favorites—and it carries an impor-tant lesson of etiquette for all hikers. Bedrock and large stones can sustain a lot of foot traf-fic, so whenever you're hiking off-trail in open environments, stay off all vegetation and exposed soil by walking only on unvegetated bedrock or by rock-hopping from stone to stone. This is a lesson that should be taught to all children, who will quickly embrace the challenge of stepping from rock to rock—similar to the game "don't step on a crack"—and eventually will incorporate it as a habit of hiking. It will be interesting to see what will happen to Mount Welch's outcrop islands if revegetation covers and hides their stone rings. My guess is that people will again stride across them once the power of the protective ring is lost.

Continuing up from this first exposed ledge on Mount Welch, the trail again becomes more defined and the impact of foot traffic lessens. The path winds through pocket forests of red oak, white pine, red maple, red spruce, paper birch, and shad, frequently opening onto floors of granite framed by outcrop communities of moss, lichen, and heath. Being on the south side of the mountain, some of the granite sections are steep due to glaciation and covered only with crustose lichen and black stains from the cyanobacteria that thrive where water frequently flows over the bedrock. On some of these steeper sections water flowing over the rock has eroded lines of weakness in the granite, creating a series of small, round depressions filled with sand. When the volume of water flowing over the granite—from either snowmelt or heavy rains—is large enough, it fills the depressions and creates whirlpools that drill farther into the granite, making mini potholes.

During my first ascent of Mount Welch Nat showed me another intriguing geological feature. It was a fairly good-sized exposed granite slab, where a portion of the surface granite had bulged upward, having been released from the underlying bedrock along an expansion joint. The result was that the one-foot-thick surface slab formed a continuous gentle dome, creating a mini cavern underneath. What caused the top foot of granite to expand and break away like this remains a puzzle to me. It is the only time I've ever seen this phenomenon.

As you ascend Mount Welch's granite ledges to about two thousand feet in elevation, a new species of tree emerges—jack pine. The northernmost species of pine in North America, this tree is uncommon in New Hampshire and reaches the southern tip of its range in New England on this mountain. The jack pine on Mount Welch grows as an open, sprawling, small tree, reaching heights between five and fifteen feet. Near the summit it takes on a more wind-contorted, bonsai form. The only other well-developed community of jack pine that I have visited in New Hampshire is on another granite dome close to Welch and Dickey—Mount Chocorua.

MOUNT CHOCORUA

At less than thirty-five hundred feet, Chocorua is smaller than more than sixty summits in the White Mountains, and yet it is one of the most climbed and easily the most photographed mountain in the region. Once again, this is not an accident, but is directly related to its exposed granite—the most extensive anywhere in New England outside Acadia National Park.

The bulk of the jack pine on Mount Chocorua grows on the northern ridge, known as the Three Sisters for its lesser summits. Chocorua's jack pine differs from Welch's in one significant way: On Mount Chocorua the jack pines display very high levels of cone serotiny (cones that won't open until heated to more than 120 degrees Fahrenheit). On one limb that was four feet in length I counted fifty-four serotinous cones. On Mount Welch only a couple of serotinous cones would be found on a limb of this age. A high proportion of serotinous cones in jack pine usually suggests that the population exists in a fire-frequent site. And this could be the case, since Chocorua is taller than any mountain within a distance of five miles, while behind Mount Welch rises a series of higher summits. Mount Chocorua would certainly be more vulnerable to lightning strikes. The problem with a fire-frequency theory is that on these exposed mountains fuel accumulates very slowly, so even with frequent lightning strikes, fires hot enough to open serotinous cones would happen at a rate of far less than one a century—not frequent enough to make serotiny an adaptive advantage. This suggests that the ancestors of Chocorua's jack pines originally existed in an environment where fire frequency was high—most likely lower-elevation areas during an earlier period of our present interglacial—while the ancestors of those on Welch existed in less fire-frequent environments.

This fire-born dome also displays dramatic relief. Chocorua's summit stands at the center of a large horseshoe-shaped ridge that opens to the east. Within this horseshoe once existed alpine glaciers that carved a large *cirque* with a steep headwall culminating in the mountain's summit dome. Due east of the summit the headwall drops a steep fifteen hundred feet. Chocorua is famous among the White Mountains because of its dramatic profile, not to mention the legend that gave the mountain its name.

Chocorua was a chief of the Pigwackets, whose tribal homeland was the Saco River watershed. In the late 1600s he befriended the family of Cornelius Campbell and, during an excursion north, left his son in Campbell's care. The boy accidentally died during Chocorua's absence. Blaming Campbell, Chocorua supposedly took revenge by killing the settler's wife and children. Legend has it that Campbell pursued Chocorua to the summit of the now famous mountain. Unwilling to allow himself to be captured, Chocorua jumped to his death off the dome's eastern headwall. There's no doubt that a jump off this summit would be fatal, but if I were being pursued, I'm not convinced I'd run up a mountain and traverse a ridge with miles of open exposed ledge.

THE GRANITE STATE

Both Chocorua and Welch are composed of Conway granite, a light-colored, medium-grained rock that underlies the White Mountains and other regions of New Hampshire, giving the state its nickname — the Granite State. Originally it was believed that this granite was a result of the Acadian Orogeny that created the granites of Mount Desert Island, but the White Mountains' granite is less than half of the age of Acadia's. Since the Acadian Orogeny there has been no subduction in the New England region, so what could have given rise to New Hampshire's much younger granite?

The answer may lie in a huge seamount that rises from the ocean floor to the east of Bermuda. Discovered by an oceanographic vessel using a fathometer in 1937, the seamount was named Great Meteor, after the boat. The Great Meteor Seamount rises more than three miles above the *abyssal plain* and has a diameter of six hundred miles. At the time no one could explain why this huge feature existed in what people had thought should be a flat ocean basin. Today it's believed that the Great Meteor Seamount is the result of a *hot spot* —

an area of the Earth under which lies an isolated mantle plume. Unlike a long rifting zone between two plates, a hot spot sits off by itself, creating a circular area of volcanic activity and associated uplift.

Many island archipelagos are the result of an oceanic plate passing over a hot spot. This is the case with the Hawaiian and Galapagos Islands. An island is formed directly above the hot spot due to uplift and volcanic activity. As the plate migrates, it carries the island away from the hot spot; in a few million years erosion reduces the island to an underwater seamount. Both the Hawaiian and Galapagos Archipelagos trail away into islands that grow smaller and smaller until they are eventually replaced by a line of seamounts.

There is evidence suggesting that about two hundred million years ago the Great Meteor Hot Spot lay under the Canadian Shield of Canada's Northwest Territories. As the North American Plate migrated in a northwesterly direction over the hot spot, the Great Meteor came to lie beneath the western shore of Hudson Bay and then, about 120 million years ago, under New Hampshire. This is similar to the age of the White Mountains' granites. Off the New England coast on the Sohm Abyssal Plain are the New England Seamounts, which trace a straight line between New Hampshire and the Great Meteor Seamount. The New England Seamounts decrease in age as they approach Great Meteor. This suggests that the young granites of the White Mountains were created as New Hampshire drifted over the Great Meteor Hot Spot during the early Cretaceous period, when dinosaurs roamed the New England landscape. The hot mantle plume melted the existing bedrock to create the granite batholith that now underlies the White Mountains.

SOUTH BALDFACE

A dramatic, exposed section of the White Mountain batholith can be found on South Baldface Mountain, which lies four miles west of the New Hampshire–Maine border. This mountain also supports the most beautiful and extensive mats of outcrop vegetation of any granite dome in the northeastern states. As on Mount Welch, the hike up South Baldface is at first gentle, but just beyond South Baldface Shelter a granite ledge rises abruptly. My most recent ascent of South Baldface was in late August 2000, following one of the wettest summers that central New England has ever experienced.

One-tenth of a mile from the shelter I leave a forest of maple, birch, and beech as I step onto a steep, smooth slab of white granite. Ice creep has kept the slab free of vegetation for more than a hundred feet in front of me. Where temporary rivulets flow over the slab, cyanobacteria, crustose lichens, and funaria create intricate weavings. Then the mountain climbs even more steeply in a long series of six-foot-high steps created by glacial quarrying. I remember a past climb up this section in the rain—it was dangerous. Today I don't need to concentrate on my footing and begin a leisurely exploration.

I work my way up the slab to the first step. A series of round holes about two inches deep at the lip of the step tells me that following the glacier's work, humans quarried here, too. Since I'm almost four miles from the nearest road and can't find any rejected pieces of granite, I guess that the quarried stone was used locally in trail construction. Up above me I see some steps with graceful, rounded lips, like the edge of a porcelain sink. These ledges were reworked by glacial ice long after neighboring blocks of bedrock were removed by glacial quarrying. As I climb each step, I see some of the most wonderful outcrop communities I have ever found on granite. For the next half mile granite ledge upon granite ledge is graced with an ever-changing array of alpine heaths and larger berry-producing shrubs. And due to the very wet summer, all are heavily laden with plump, juicy berries.

A number of people have hiked up today to pick low-bush blueberries, which are at their prime. But tasty bog bilberry and black crowberry are also abundant, as are the tart mountain cranberries. The steep, challenging trail keeps people from wandering, so the vegetated granite steps are wonderfully intact. But today I am here to photograph these outcrop communities. Stepping carefully to place my feet only on granite, I meander across numerous steps, some only a few feet in width, others creating shelves as wide as a highway.

A crevice community with mountain cranberry

I begin to see a pattern in the composition of crevice communities as I climb. Those most exposed to the wind are dominated by mountain cranberry, black crowberry, three-toothed cinquefoil, and alpine reindeer lichen. The interplay of colors from the bright red cranberries to the black crowberries, intermixed with clumps of light green alpine reindeer lichen, is striking. The mountain cranberry is a handsome plant. Along with its brilliant berries, it has small, shiny leaves, cleft down the middle by a single midrib. The thick, waxy cuticle on the cranberry leaves protects against desiccation from dry winter winds.

In crevices a bit more wind protected, low-bush blueberry and bog bilberry dominate—each holding similar sky-blue berries. Tucked against the back of each step, sheep laurel, Labrador tea, and bunchberry thrive. And in the most wind-protected depressions I find rhodora, mountain holly, wild raisin, and American mountain ash. It is obvious that all these communities have existed here, untrammeled, for a long time. Under the canopy of the various shrubs is a complete carpet of alpine reindeer lichen—all haircap moss has long since been excluded by the lichen. This is an indication that, successionally, these communities are old.

The larger shrubs—mountain holly, wild raisin, and mountain ash—are in full berry, too. Although the holly produces the fewest berries, they are the most beautiful—a rich purplish red. The wild raisin and mountain ash are bent under the weight of their respective black and red berry clusters. All these berries create an artist's palette of color, making this a glorious time of year to visit South Baldface, though two other times are equally compelling— late June and late September.

In late June all these shrubs are in full bloom, with the most dramatic being rhodora. Rhodora is a member of the heath family most closely related to rhododendron, and as such bears large purple blooms. On South Baldface and its sister mountain, North Baldface, rhodora grows in the largest and densest colonies that I have ever seen. During a good bloom year the Baldfaces' stands of rhodora can be spellbinding.

Yet I think my favorite time to make a visit to South Baldface is at the close of September, when the leaves of all these shrubs turn various shades of reds and purples. The bog bilberry is most captivating. It turns an astounding shade of luminous bluish purple, making the alpine zone where it occurs in the White Mountains every bit as impressive as the slopes cloaked with vibrant yellows and reds from the leaves of birches and maples. Both the purple of the bilberry and red of the maple are the result of the production of *anthocyanin*. Anthocyanin is a pigment that absorbs infrared (a fancy term for "heat"), making its presence a good attribute for plants that grow in cold climates. As leaves stop producing chlorophyll during the fall, bilberries and maples convert sugar into anthocyanin. A plant's internal pH dictates the shade of this pigment. In acidic leaves such as those of red maple this pigment is bright red, but in the more alkaline foliage of the bilberry, it is purple. September is also a time when clouds catch these granite domes, making all their fall colors almost iridescent.

While not bathed in fog today, these outcrop species invite me to get down on hands and knees to explore their intricacies. On close inspection, black crowberry is most intriguing to me. This species looks like a kind of sprawling moss. It has tiny, evergreen leaves—smaller than uncooked grains of rice—and yet it is a diminutive flowering shrub. It produces edible black berries each the size of a pea, which are not easy to pick out from the plant's dark foliage in fall. This raises a question: When most berry-producing plants advertise their fruits with bright colors so that animals can easily find them to disperse their seeds, why does black crowberry have

Black crowberry

fruits that are difficult to see? I don't have the answer, but I'd guess the crowberry relies on mammals, whose sense of smell is far more developed than their vision, to disperse its seeds.

After half a mile of climbing and more than an hour of exploration, I find that the granite steps level out, and I crest a north-facing ridge that ramps up toward the summit of South Baldface. Here the granite has been broken by the harsh climate, which has also eliminated the larger shrubs. I now stand in the midst of alpine tundra cloaked in low mats of bilberry, crowberry, and three-toothed cinquefoil. For the next four miles, as I hike the trail that loops over both South and North Baldface, I climb in and out of heath-dominated communities that have colonized exposed granite. All of them are robustly vegetated, with the exception of one terrace—the site of a trail junction about half a mile east of the summit of South Baldface. As I gaze down on this spot from the mountain's summit, I hope that the impact doesn't expand, so that for generations to come this mountain will represent the very best that an eastern granite dome can offer.

THE ADIRONDACKS

West of the White Mountains are the Adirondacks, with very similar granite outcrop communities. While the Whites have some of the youngest granites found in our northern states, the Adirondacks have the oldest, at more than a billion years. All the other granite domes covered in this book were formed from magma, but the granite of the Adirondacks was formed from existing bedrock that wasn't heated to the point of complete melting. This can be seen in the faint parallel lines of crystals that run through the granite, suggesting the original bedding planes of the ancient bedrock. The origins of this metamorphosed granite are not well understood, nor is the fact that the Adirondacks are currently experiencing uplift, making this one of the most seismically active regions in the northeastern states. Of this I have personal experience.

During the fall of 1983 I was beginning my second year as a teacher at the Putney School. I was living in one of the school's dorms, and before sunrise on October 7, I experienced something unusual. I awoke out of a sound sleep to a chorus of crickets (common on warm New England fall nights) resonating through our bedroom window. And then, without warning, all the crickets stopped at exactly the same time. As I was contemplating how strange it was that all the crickets would stop at once, I began to hear rumbling that sounded something like an approaching truck. Our room began to shake as the noise increased until it sounded as if the large truck had slammed into the side of the dorm. The noise and rumbling quickly subsided, and within a couple of minutes the chorus of crickets resumed. What I had experienced was a rare New England earthquake, a respectable 5.2 trembler with its epicenter in the Adirondacks 150 miles away—a result of the region's uplift. What is causing the Adirondacks to grow at this time is not clear, but this circular range of mountains may be heralding the birth of a new hot spot.

The ecologies of the Adirondacks and the White Mountains are quite similar. Both have exposed granite summits between three and four thousand feet, which host nearly identical outcrop communities. But there is one big difference between the granite balds of these two mountainous areas—the amount of jointing in the rock surface. The Adirondacks' granite is dramatically dissected by joints that resemble diagrams of the human vascular system. Since this metamorphosed granite never completely melted, the pressure associated with its formation fractured the existing bedrock. The result is that few expanses of clean, smooth granite occur naturally in the Adirondacks—crevice communities abound. At the same time, as on Mount Welch, hiking pressure on many of these peaks has dramatically exposed the once cloaked bedrock.

This is obvious on a loop hike that takes me over Noonmark and Round Mountains. Like Chocorua in the Whites, Noonmark is one of the most climbed Adirondack summits, even though it is less than four thousand feet. A steep two-mile hike brings me to the top of this mountain, which lies on the eastern side of the High Peaks Wilderness. The exposed bedrock on the summit is relatively level, about an acre in size, and drops off steeply on all sides.

Today roughly 25 percent of the summit area is covered by outcrop vegetation, but one hundred years ago that coverage would have been more like 75 percent. In one area the glacier removed a three-foot-thick section of granite, creating an alcove about thirty feet square. On the alcove's granite walls lichens cover the top two feet and then abruptly stop, creating an obvious line. This shows that at one time the entire alcove was vegetated with more than a foot of soil. Trampling of the fragile crowberry and heaths created footpaths that eventually expanded through erosion until everything was washed away. Even in the White Mountains, I've never witnessed this degree of impact. Everywhere I look on Noonmark's summit, I see apparitions of the outcrop communities that once existed.

I proceed down the north side of Noonmark and climb to the three-thousand-foot summit of Round Mountain—named for its classic dome shape. A lesser peak with more limited views, Round Mountain receives fewer hikers, and the difference in vegetation is noticeable. This summit is not free of hiker impact, but the impact is concentrated along the trail. Within a few strides of either side of the trail, I easily find intact outcrop communities. The result is that Round Mountain has an unforested summit with scattered tree islands, but exposed granite comprises less than a quarter of the area, forming small openings here and there—a picture of what Noonmark may have looked like a century ago.

I am completing the day's loop, and the last mile and a half takes me through an impressive old-growth forest of hemlock and some sugar maple. The old growth is spread across a steep north-facing slope that is protected from the wind. Hundreds of hemlocks and a host of maples more than three feet in diameter grace the trail as it meanders down shelves in the ravine wall. A forest such as this simply doesn't exist in the White Mountains, where everything below thirty-five hundred feet was logged in the late nineteenth and early twentieth centuries. In New Hampshire an old-growth stand of this size would be big news. In the protected Adirondack Park, where old growth is more common, this stand probably receives no special recognition.

The old-growth forest stands in dramatic contrast to Noonmark's summit. Only a needle-covered trail indicates that humans have been here, while on Noonmark evidence of people is everywhere, including lots of litter (enough to fill a large plastic bag). If we consider that a patch of black crowberry two feet in diameter is close to a century in age, then the outcrop communities that once occurred on Noonmark were old growth, too, taking centuries or millennia to form on this glaciated granite. As people who love these mountains, we need to develop a new awareness that age is not related to size. On these northeastern mountain balds, delicate, low-lying outcrop communities deserve the same level of respect and reverence that we have for the towering forests of similar age.

Clear Lake backed by Steeple and Temple Peaks, Wind River Range

CHAPTER SEVEN

The Wind Rivers:
Temples of Stone

Right in the middle of America's Continental Divide, between the Rocky Mountains of northern New Mexico and the dramatic ranges of Glacier National Park, are the Wind Rivers—the roof of Wyoming. The Wind River Range runs about one hundred miles from southeast to northwest, mimicking the general direction of the Rocky Mountains from New Mexico to Canada. A soaring island surrounded on three sides by high prairie and desert, the Wind Rivers host Wyoming's highest peaks and more summits over twelve thousand feet than any other range in the state. Their rugged relief and numerous alpine lakes are a big draw for wilderness enthusiasts. On their southern flanks the Oregon Trail crossed the divide at South Pass. Could the pioneers of John Bidwell's 1841 wagon train (the first to make the journey) have been prepared for the Wind Rivers, snowcapped peaks soaring more than a mile above Wyoming's high plains?

Thoughts such as these are constant companions as I drive across Nebraska on Interstate 80 during the summer of 1999. Lewis and Clark, the Oregon Trail, the first half of the nineteenth century—it all seems so distant. Yet my grandfather, whom I knew and loved as a child, was born in 1880. His father was born in 1840. Thus it's possible that my great-grandfather, as an infant, could have been a member of Bidwell's party. In this context the pioneer history of the West doesn't seem so remote.

A couple of hundred miles to the north lies Wounded Knee. The massacre of Big Foot's band of Sioux occurred there in 1890, just sixty years before my birth. In a decade I'll be closing in on that number of years. Yet here I drive at a speed of seventy miles an hour, passing in rapid succession the sites where pioneer forts once stood. To make it from Fort Kearney to Fort McPherson would have taken a wagon train many days, but I'm able to click off the distance in a little more than an hour.

How could so much change occur in such a short span of time? When my great-grandfather was a young boy, this land was devoid of ranches, fencing, roads, and power lines. Bison, too numerous to count, roamed its prairies. If I had been born just a few generations earlier, I could have experienced this western prairie as untamed wilderness—a landscape now dissected and bound by straight lines of various types. But luckily, in the Wind River backcountry the landscape looks much as it did when Bidwell's group crossed the Continental Divide at South Pass.

My first excursion into the Wind Rivers begins at Big Sandy—the most remote trailhead in these mountains. Once I turn off Route 191, I drive about forty miles on dirt roads before beginning my hike. Remote it may be, yet Big Sandy is one of the most popular trailheads into the Bridger Wilderness, which dominates the western side of the range. A two-hour ride over continuous washboard is not a deterrent to people seeking this point of entry into the Wind Rivers. The reason soon becomes clear.

Just a few minutes after I leave the trailhead, I am walking through glorious, wildflower-filled intervales lining the Big Sandy River. A decade has passed since my last backcountry experience in the Rockies, and I find myself startled by the beautiful mixture of river, intervale, lodgepole pine forest, and upland glades. If not for the swarms of mosquitoes (which I battle continuously for the next four weeks), I'd stop and reflect on the idyllic beauty of this valley. But my destination is the granite balds that lie to the southeast of Big Sandy Lake—another eight miles up the trail.

At ninety-seven hundred feet, Big Sandy Lake sits at the junction of four prominent glacial valleys. Picture a gentle lake surrounded by lush, grassy, wildflower-studded meadows that gently rise toward a fringe of lodgepole pine and Engelmann spruce forest. The forest backs onto outcroppings of granite. Beyond the outcroppings open the mouths of steep U-shaped valleys framed by walls of clean, shining, exfoliated granite rising almost two thousand vertical feet toward the Continental Divide. Each valley displays the classic features left by alpine glaciers. Everywhere above ten thousand feet the Wind River batholith lies exposed through the surgical cutting of glacial ice. This ancient granite — the basement of the ancestral Rocky Mountains — was formed in the Helikian period of the Precambrian, 1.4 billion years ago. And now it frames the spectacular relief that radiates out from the lake.

RISE AND FALL OF THE ROCKIES

The Wind Rivers, along with the other Rocky Mountain ranges, represent one of today's most puzzling geological problems. Lying close to a thousand miles from the boundary of the Pacific and North American Plates, how could these mountains — rising almost three miles above sea level — have been formed? Although plate tectonic theory is readily accepted as the explanation for mountain building across the globe, it runs into problems in the Rockies. Geologically speaking, the Rockies are young, and yet they lie far from any zone of plate collision or subduction. To examine theories attempting to explain the origins of the Rocky Mountains, let's go back to the Helikian period.

In the middle of this geological period and more than one billion years before plants and animals were able to colonize the land, the coastline of what is now the western United States was almost a thousand miles farther east — close to the current Idaho-Wyoming border. Inland from this coastline, through present-day Wyoming and Montana, imagine extensive flat plains similar to those found in Iowa or Kansas. But these plains were not covered with fields of corn or wheat; they were devoid of plants, their dust-covered surfaces dissected by fishless rivers.

Subduction commencing about 1.4 billion years ago warped this part of the continent, building the lifeless ancestral Rocky Mountains. At their heart, more than six miles below the Earth's surface, a huge granite batholith formed. Long before the end of the Helikian period, the ancestral Rockies eroded to the sea and the batholith lay covered by thousands of feet of eroded mountain sediments. The land would remain relatively quiet for more than a billion years.

Then, just prior to the departure of the dinosaurs about seventy million years ago, the Rockies rose a second time in what is called the Laramide Orogeny. First, thousands of feet of sedimentary rock was warped upward to create a highland. At that time the climate in Wyoming was similar to Florida's, so it didn't take long for frequent cloudbursts to remove the sedimentary rock—leaving a series of ranges that, fifty million years ago, looked quite similar to the Rockies we see today. Next, millions of years of erosion reduced these mountains and buried them in their own sediments. By ten million years ago only the highest peaks rose a thousand feet or so above a flat plain that covered more than 90 percent of Wyoming.

When a third period of uplift occurred during the past ten million years, the Rockies rose more than a mile in elevation, and once again sediments were stripped from their sides to create the mountainous landscape we see today. But what could have caused the Laramide Orogeny seventy million years ago, or the more recent uplift that took place in the past ten million years?

When an oceanic plate collides with a continental plate, the higher-density oceanic crust is forced beneath the continental crust in what is called subduction. It's believed that the oceanic crust dives at a steep angle, resulting in uplift and mountain building within a couple of hundred miles of the plate boundary. This is what built the ancestral Rocky Mountains during the Helikian period. But if the continental crust adjacent to a subduction zone is not very thick, the oceanic crust might subduct at a low angle. This would carry the oceanic crust far inland beneath the continent before it reached depths hot enough to melt it, creating magma and associated mountain building. Low-angle subduction is the theory currently believed to explain the Laramide Orogeny, since seventy million years ago the continent west of the Rockies was devoid of mountains — a flat marshy plain extending to the Pacific. At that time the western continental crust was thin. However, during the most recent period of Rocky Mountain uplift — less than ten million years ago — the Sierra Nevada was growing, with the continental crust beneath it reaching great depths. This would have restricted low-level subduction. So what brought about this recent, third period of uplift that removed thousands of feet of sediment to expose once again the rugged Rockies and their ancient granites?

In the previous chapter I mentioned that the White Mountain granites of New Hampshire puzzled geologists, because they are too young to be explained by the Acadian Orogeny. But the migration of New Hampshire over the Great Meteor Hot Spot might explain the origin of that young batholith. The recent uplift of the northern Rockies also might be explained by the migration of North America over another hot spot, which is currently centered beneath Yellowstone National Park. North America has been drifting westward at an average rate of a couple of centimeters a year. Ten million years ago the Yellowstone hot spot lay under Idaho. As the continent drifted over this hot spot, upwelling of magma in the northern Rocky Mountain region could have generated uplift, exposing the granites that now frame the roof of the Wind Rivers and other ranges of the Rockies. If this is the case, in another twenty million years the plains of the Dakotas will be replaced by mountains.

Whether or not low-angle subduction and the migration of hot spots are in fact the processes that created these mountains, recent glaciation has clearly left its mark. Twenty thousand years ago the ice in this portion of the Wind Rivers covered everything between 9,000 and 11,500 feet. All the granite within this range of elevation was sculpted into domes, whereas higher granites took on the dramatic relief created by alpine glaciers: Continental glaciers reduce regional relief, but alpine glaciers accentuate it. In the northeastern United States gla-cial ice completely cloaked all but the highest mountains, making features carved by alpine glaciers rare. But in the valleys radiating out from Big Sandy Lake, cirques, horns, arêtes, and glacial stairways abound.

An alpine glacier is birthed on the side of a mountain as accumulating snow is compressed to ice and reaches depths of sixty meters. Under great weight, the glacial ice becomes plastic and starts to flow down the slope, carving into the mountain as it moves. But the ice doesn't flow like a stream, cutting a long narrow valley. Instead, as more snow accumulates on the glacier's upper elevations, the glacier rotates around its center and, like a rounded rasp, carves farther into the mountain. To visualize this process, imagine that you are at the beach and you've made a five-foot-high mountain out of sand. Along with shovels and buck-ets you just happen to have a beach ball with a rough surface. If you place the ball on the side of your mountain and slowly rotate it downward, it will start to carve into the side of your mountain, creating a bowl-shaped depression. This is similar to the way an alpine glacier carves a steep-walled, bowl-shaped valley called a cirque. If the snow accumulates faster than the ice is melting at the glacier's snout, the glacier will flow out of its cirque and farther down the mountain, cutting a steep-walled, U-shaped valley. But unlike a U-shaped notch carved by a continental glacier, this alpine valley will be carved into what is called a glacial stair-way—a series of large steps on the floor of the valley, each holding a glacial lake called a *tarn*. It's unclear why alpine glaciers carve stairways, though the phenomenon is probably related to zones of increased pressure within the glacier, which produce more meltwater and, as a result, greater quarrying.

Where two cirques cut into a mountain on either side of a ridge and begin to merge, a steep-sided, knife-edge ridge called an *arête* is formed between them. Where three or more alpine glaciers cut into a mountain, a towering spirelike summit called a *horn* can be produced. As I hike from Big Sandy Lake up a glacial stairway toward Deep Lake, cirques, arêtes, and horns frame the dramatic relief that surrounds me.

A glaciated alpine valley with a glacial stairway, arêtes, and a horn

Between Clear and Deep Lakes I step onto an extensive floor of glaciated granite. The braided stream flowing between the two tarns removed all soil and till, leaving a streambed close to two hundred feet wide composed solely of clean, granite bedrock. I've hiked across granite streambeds in New Hampshire's White Mountains, but they're rarely wider than fifty feet. In the middle of this drainage I encounter an island of granite about a hundred feet wide and three hundred feet long, framed by the parting of the stream. Following seasonal flooding, the slab is completely devoid of any plant growth—even lichens and cyanobacteria. Although this bedrock is ancient, not a single joint breaks its thirty-thousand-square-foot surface. If the Earth's crust can be thought of as skin, then this is the skin of a newborn. I've never encountered such an extensive smooth, clean slab of granite—one that lay in its mountain womb for 1.4 billion years and was birthed through glaciation just a few millennia ago.

Mosquitoes or not, I'm compelled to stop on its elegant surface. I pull out my netted shirt (complete with zippered hood), put on my gloves, and lie down. I feel the granite's cold against my back as I listen to the rushing of the stream and examine, through a cloud of mosquitoes, the eastern arête rise a vertical quarter of a mile toward the summit of Haystack Mountain. There is a distinct change in the exposed granite on the arête's face at about 11,500 feet. Below this elevation the surface of the granite is smooth and light in color, like the bedrock on which I lie, but above this elevation the surface displays gentler relief, is broken into blocks of many sizes, and is much darker in color. What could be responsible for such a striking change? It appears that the upper portion was never covered by glacial ice and has been weathered by the fierce Wind River climate for tens of thousands of years.

Two miles farther to the south rises Steeple Peak, an impressive, aptly named twelve-hundred-foot horn. Steeple Peak and Haystack Mountain, never being covered by glacial ice, are *nunataks*—islands of rock poking through the glacial ice and serving as refuges for alpine species during periods of glaciation. To the west lies a beautiful dome with an eleven-thousand-foot summit—my quest for the day. And to the south of it stands Temple Peak. Reposing on the granite, I imagine that I lie upon the polished floor of a massive, roofless cathedral. Given the names of the surrounding peaks, it appears I'm not the first person to think this.

As I eat lunch on my island of granite, I notice the clouds growing larger to the west. Thunderstorms in the Rockies develop with amazing speed, so I decide to work my way to the top of the dome quickly before lightning forces me to retreat. I leave the streambed and walk through glorious islands of tall Engelmann spruce, which has colonized the glaciated granite. The islands resemble candelabras: The trees at the center are the tallest, steadily decreasing in height toward the perimeter. Anxious to summit the dome, I don't take the time to see whether this is the result of younger trees colonizing the perimeter of the islands as they expanded outward, or the trees are clones produced through *layering*.

A number of conifers have the ability to layer—a process in which the lower living branches that come into contact with the ground can grow roots and sprout new vertical growth, creating a grove of trees that are in fact a single individual. Through layering, spruce in the alpine zone of the Rockies can migrate across the landscape. When I first heard this as a graduate student in an alpine ecology course, I was shocked—migrating trees! During winter the trees are ice-blasted and killed back on their windward sides, whereas in summer they layer and grow out on their wind-protected, leeward sides. In time the wind-exposed trunk can be killed by repeated ice-blasting, setting the tree free of its original root system. A tree can migrate hundreds of meters across the alpine tundra through centuries of ice-blasting and layering if it doesn't encounter a rock outcrop or glacial boulder. When this happens its ability to layer ceases, and eventually it is ice-blasted out of existence.

As I work my way up the northeastern face of the dome, the coarse, gray granite remains free of joints, but I begin to encounter exquisite round depression communities a few feet in diameter. Wherever the glacier has gouged a slight depression in the granite, coarse sands

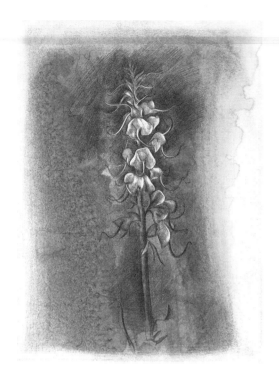

Purple elephant head

have accumulated and been colonized by an amazing array of alpine wildflowers. If there is a single feature that most separates the alpine zone of western mountains from those of the East, it is the opulent bloom of the western alpine. But I wasn't expecting to witness such a dramatic display on exposed granite. Within the depression communities are purple elephant head, red Indian paintbrush, white American bistort, yellow wallflower, pink mountain heather, and deep blue violet—a brilliant, jumbled rainbow of color.

Of all these flowers, the elephant head is the most intriguing. Why would a plant produce flowers that strikingly resemble the head of an African elephant? It's not uncommon to see forms repeated in nature—fractals being an example—but flowers with large earlike petals and long curving trunks? In fact, what looks like an elephant's head is actually a shape perfectly structured to accommodate bumblebee pollinators. When a bee lands on one of the flowers and crawls partially into the elephant head's mouth to harvest nectar, the earlike petals hold the bee's body in just the right position to allow its back to be dusted with pollen. And the tip of the trunk, which holds the flower's female stigma, is precisely long enough to touch the bee's back where pollen from previous flower visits has been placed, completing cross-pollination.

The clouds growing dark and ominous in the west push me onward. Now the side of the dome grows steeper and the depression communities vanish, as does all lichen growth. At this angle of repose, ice creep keeps the granite as clean as the rushing waters sweep smooth the island of granite four hundred feet below me. I'm wondering what my traction will be like if I need to descend this portion of the dome in the rain; I pick up my pace. As I approach the summit, the granite levels out and becomes carpeted with lichens. This is my first encounter with lichen-covered bedrock on a Wind River dome.

With no ice creep or flowing water, the lichen coverage is close to 100 percent. Yet the only lichens present are crustose, mostly species of gray lecanora and green map lichen. I know that few people venture up here to tramp around the summit, preferring instead to follow the trail up the valley to Temple Pass. So the lack of foliose lichen can't be due to foot traffic. I notice that the crevice communities are dominated by moss campion. This dwarf alpine plant grows as a dense mat no more than a centimeter in height with tightly packed leaves smaller than grains of rice—adaptations that allow it to grow in extreme winds. I guess the lack of foliose lichen, and most vegetation other than moss campion, is due to strong winds and associated winter ice-blasting.

Moss campion often dominates Rocky Mountain *fellfield* communities. *Fell* is a European word for "stone," so a fellfield is an area of the alpine zone with about half its surface covered with stones. Fellfields are products of high winds that carry away fine materials and restrict plant growth. So the large amount of moss campion in the crevice communities here indicates that a prominent force on this dome's summit is wind—one that is now really picking up. Still, I have to get down on my hands and knees and marvel at these dwarfed dense mats, which are completely covered with delicate pink, bell-shaped flowers. In this wind-stressed environment I'm inspired by the way this tough ground-hugging plant can produce such an opulent bloom—one that is at any minute going to experience the full brunt of the storm.

Thinking that I won't make it down before the storm breaks, I work my way south to a col in the dome's ridgeline as the buffeting wind starts to affect my balance. I duck into a stand of Engelmann spruce and limber pine, their dwarfed forms reminiscent of pitch pine groves found on eastern balds. Limber is the most wind-hardy pine in the Wind Rivers, and the only one able to venture above the tree line. I huddle under a pine with my back against a wall of granite quarried by the glaciers as hail starts to rain down. Lightning flashes in the south. I count eight seconds before thunder echoes down the valley and rides over me—the right direction and distance for a direct strike on the Steeple's spire. I'm thankful for the protection the quarried col offers.

The power, intensity, and speed of a Rocky Mountain thunderstorm are something to behold, and I'm reminded of John Muir climbing to the top of a pine to feel the full impact of one. With lightening hitting the rimrock at a rate of more than one strike per minute, the crackle of thunder just seconds away, and the hail changing to pelting rain, I'm not compelled to follow Muir's example. I stay huddled for the next half hour, feeling quite protected by granite, spruce, and pine.

With the exception of the wind-exposed, dry summit of the dome, the rain reminds me that the flora I've encountered throughout the day is typical of wet alpine conditions. Obviously, this section of the Continental Divide captures a lot of the water that washes over the granites of this valley. This is markedly different from what I find on the granite domes surrounding Senaca Lake, which lies forty miles to the northwest.

SENACA LAKE

To get to Senaca Lake, I hike out of Elkhart Park through miles of lodgepole pine. My first view of this area's granite domes comes at an overlook appropriately called Photographers Point. Stretching eastward for five miles before me—twice this distance to the north and south—is an extensive series of domes that were completely covered by glacial ice only ten thousand years ago. Behind them, about eight miles distant, are the nunataks of the Continental Divide. The difference between the landscape once covered by ice and the peaks that poked through it is striking. The land in front of me rolls gently like swells on a glassy sea and then, as it reaches the glaciers and snowfields of the high peaks, dramatically piles up like breakers capped by white foam. This is the first time in my life that I feel the magnitude of the Pleistocene glaciations. Scanning the region in front of me, I can clearly see an area close to a hundred square miles that was once completely hidden under glacial ice. In New England everything I observe was once cloaked in ice, making it harder to perceive the extent of coverage. But here, in this section of the Wind Rivers, the area of coverage stands out. From my perspective, it is immense. Yet I know it is nothing compared to the coverage of the Laurentide Ice Sheet. To confirm my epiphany, I look at my Rand McNally Road Atlas map of the United States when I return to my truck. This hundred-square-mile area isn't even as big as the head of a pin on my map. That the Laurentide Ice Sheet covered an area of North America at least thirty thousand times larger is a powerful realization.

Looking over the landscape from Photographers Point, I decide to explore two domes that lie to the east of Senaca Lake. On my map they both top out at a bit more than eleven thousand feet. As I hike the three miles between the point and the domes, it becomes obvious that this landscape is drier than the Big Sandy Lake region. Fire has left its mark throughout the area. I turn left off the trail to bushwhack to the first dome, approaching an older stand of lodgepole pine recently killed by fire. The trees have shed their bark, and their trunks display tight spiral growth. All trees have some degree of genetically determined spiraling, but the environment, particularly wind, decides how tight each tree's spiral will be. Can you guess how the wind does this? Trees growing in wind-protected sites can vigorously grow upward, stretching their spirals, while trees in wind-exposed sites elongate slowly, generating tight spirals. The tight spiral is a distinct advantage for wind-exposed trees, since it makes their trunks stronger. It is a marvelously malleable adaptation: The environment dictates the exact degree of spiraling needed for each individual's survival in its particular conditions.

When I step onto granite ledge, I find none of the moist depression communities that I saw on the dome between Deep and Clear Lakes. Here shrubby cinquefoil, yarrow, and goldenrod dominate crevice communities—all drier-sited species than elephant head, pink heather,

A spiral-trunked lodgepole pine snag

and violet. This is puzzling given that the granite around Senaca Lake has ample vertical joints, which could capture and hold water better than shallow depression communities. I can only assume that being about five miles farther west of the divide's high peaks, Senaca Lake receives less precipitation than Big Sandy Lake.

As I work my way up the first dome, wind-stunted limber pine colonizes pockets where glacial ice quarried the bedrock. These wind-protected depressions are usually five to six feet deep. The trees grow straight to this height and then become dramatically gnarled. These pines are ancient, with basal diameters reaching more than two feet. Since limber pine can live for a thousand years, I imagine that pines of this stature are at least half that age. Surrounding the pines are clumps of blue mertensia, white yarrow, and yellow goldenrod, providing color to the otherwise sparsely vegetated gray granite.

In terms of biotic diversity these domes are poorer than those at Big Sandy Lake. Lacking steep glacial valleys, horns, and arêtes, the landscape around Senaca Lake is also tame in comparison. But it feels more remote. For the next two days I don't encounter a single other person; I guess that the rugged high peaks have lured them farther to the east. My only companions are swarms of mosquitoes, and I find myself spending many hours in my tent reading.

After five days on my own in the Wind Rivers, particularly the last two at Senaca Lake, I'm feeling quite lonely. I'm surprised by this, since as a younger man I reveled in spending time alone in the wilderness. Now as I approach fifty years of age, something has changed—I need to share my experiences with others. I decide it's time to go.

As I depart the Wind Rivers, driving through the prairie north of Pinedale, thunderheads have blossomed over the divide and lightning pierces the veiled peaks. The Wind Rivers are a massive island—one with an almost magnetic attraction for thunderstorms. Only one out of my five days was storm-free. The rain in summer and the grinding of glaciers throughout the year are slowly but consistently washing this island of ancient granite into the surrounding prairie sea. But today, uplifted to an elevation of almost three miles by unseen forces, temporarily free of its white mantle of ice, it looks much as it did when Jim Bridger, renowned Mountain Man, explored this range in the early 1820s.

At 10,500 feet in the Beartooths

CHAPTER EIGHT

The Beartooths:
Alpine Gardens

From the Wind Rivers the Continental Divide works its way to the northwest through Yellowstone National Park. But if you travel due north from the Wind Rivers, you will cross the Absaroka and then the Beartooth Mountains. Together these three ranges form the historic boundary between two great Native American Nations—the Shoshone and the Absaroka (or Crow). The people of these tribes must have known the mountain ranges intimately, because each summer they moved their camps to higher elevations to collect berries, hunt for deer and elk, and fish mountain lakes too numerous to count. They certainly noticed how similar the Wind Rivers and Beartooths were with their exposed granite domes, and how different the Absaroka Mountains were with their young, extensive lava flows. Imagining how Native American legends might explain the origins of these very different, neighboring mountains keeps me busy as I make my way toward my next destination.

For my excursion into the Beartooths, I have the great pleasure of Rich Thompson's company— an old friend from my days at the University of Colorado. After my lonely stint in the Wind Rivers, it's good to set off with Rich up the Russell Creek drainage, named for Osborne Russell—a Mountain Man.

A nineteenth-century icon of the American West that is every bit as powerful as that of the cowboy and American Indian is the buckskin-clad Mountain Man. I had stopped at the

Museum of the Mountain Man in Pinedale, Wyoming, on my departure from the Wind Rivers and couldn't help but reflect on this brief but defining period of American history—a period focused solely on the trapping of beaver. To appreciate how a rodent dramatically impacted the opening of the West, affected the history of a fledgling nation, and created an American icon, we need to review a bit of history.

When Europeans first made voyages to eastern North America in the sixteenth century, they did so primarily to explore the New World and to conduct trade with Native Americans—furs being the preferred commodity. By the start of the seventeenth century beaver had become the most sought-after of all furs. At that time hats made from beaver pelts became an important symbol of status for European men—a social norm that would last for more than two centuries. Given the increasing demand for its pelt, the beaver was almost exterminated from all areas east of the Mississippi River by 1800. Then in 1803 Thomas Jefferson completed the Louisiana Purchase and, a year later, sent Lewis and Clark off to explore this new territory and chronicle all that they found. One of their discoveries was an abundance of beaver throughout the upper Missouri watershed.

Even before Lewis and Clark finished their journey, word of their encounters with beaver made it back east. During their return in 1806, they met two individuals heading to the Rocky Mountains to begin a fur trade with the Native peoples of that region. Being unfamiliar with the territory, the two men asked John Colter, a member of Lewis and Clark's party, if he might guide them. Colter was released from his service to the expedition to act as guide. This marked the beginning of beaver trade in the western mountains—a period that would end by 1840 as silk replaced beaver pelts as the preferred material for men's hats.

For the first sixteen years of the era, traders exchanged such goods as woven cloth, knives, and metal pots with Native Americans for beaver pelts. Then in 1822 William Ashley developed a new strategy: Rather than simply trading in furs, he hired men to roam the Rocky

Mountains and trap the beaver directly. The trappers became Mountain Men—a tough, resourceful, self-reliant group of individuals who opened the American West.

These individuals spent most of their days alone in the mountains, often going for months at a time without human contact. They had to be able to make or repair everything they owned—clothing, rifles, bullets, knives. They persevered through tough mountain conditions and hardships with no modern conveniences. (Personally, I have no idea how they survived the mosquito swarms from which my netted clothing and tent protect me.) And they had to constantly be on the lookout for attacks from grizzly bears or hostile tribes. Few made it longer than ten years as Mountain Men. Most died young, often violently. When we consider that the period of the Mountain Man lasted less than twenty years (from 1822 to 1840), and that during this time their numbers totaled only a few hundred, it's amazing that their story forged a quintessential image of the American West.

Helping foster the legend of the Mountain Men was their annual rendezvous, another brainchild of William Ashley. Rather than having the trappers return to St. Louis to unload their furs and resupply for another year, Ashley took wagon trains west once a year to carry supplies to the Mountain Men, then return to St. Louis with their furs. The first rendezvous was held in 1825, the last in 1840. These monthlong gatherings of hundreds of Mountain Men and often thousands of Native Americans became the single most important social occasion in the American West. During the rendezvous, men tested their skills against one another, traded, gambled, and told tales of epic proportions. It's these tales that have survived and sculpted the image of the Mountain Man. Although their stories were certainly inflated, these individuals lived exceedingly hard, danger-filled lives. Contemplating their experiences makes me reconsider my sense of loneliness after a few short days in the Wind Rivers.

By 1840 beaver pelts had gone out of fashion and the Mountain Men were gone, but during their short tenure they had explored every valley of the western mountains. Their endeavors paved the way for the settling of the land from the Rocky Mountains to the Pacific Coast. In the northern Rockies the settlement commenced with Bidwell's 1841 wagon-train traverse of the Oregon Trail—a route discovered by Mountain Men. So as Rich and I head up the path along Russell Creek, I realize that long before hikers cut this trail, Mountain Men, Shoshone, and Absaroka had already explored all that we would find.

About a mile up the trail we enter a lodgepole pine forest whose floor is completely covered with a healthy stand of mountain huckleberry. The leaves of this *ericaceous* shrub are an almost iridescent light green—as if the understory of this forest might glow in the dark. Only a recent fire could produce such a robust stand of huckleberry. We then encounter standing dead lodgepole snags, heat-killed by fire. We come upon a beautiful ledge of black-and-white gneiss whose folded layers swirl like some delicious flavor of Ben & Jerry's ice cream. The ledge was laid bare by fire and tantalizingly suggests the exposed balds that lie ahead. As we hike farther up Russell Creek, evidence of fire becomes more and more common, and we begin to encounter entire granite domes holding the stubble of snags that were once forests of lodgepole pine.

What Rich and I are seeing are newborn granite balds. These balds were previously cloaked in forests of lodgepole pine and, at higher elevations, Engelmann spruce and subalpine fir. The fire found its way into the crowns of the conifers, killing all of them. A year of subsequent erosion removed the soil down to bedrock, leaving scattered snags clinging to crevices. At times the fire must have been exceptionally hot, heat-killing huge spruce up to four feet in diameter. At nine thousand feet in elevation, these were ancient trees—their slow vertical growth recorded in the tight spiral pattern visible in their bare trunks.

It won't be until Rich and I depart from the Beartooths that we realize we're observing the very northeastern extent of the 1988 Yellowstone fires. As we drive through Yellowstone en route to Jackson Hole, Wyoming, the geographic scope of those fires dawns on us. Although I did research in Yellowstone in 1990, I worked in only one portion of the park and never

Conifer snags killed by the 1988 fire

grasped the full extent of the burn. But Rich and I drive for two hours, a distance of more than seventy-five miles, and evidence of the 1988 fire is with us the entire time. That these fires consumed an area equal to half my home state of Vermont is staggering. Yet fires of this magnitude probably happen once every couple of hundred years here, when exceptionally hot, dry, windy summers occur. They are simply a part of this area's ecology.

We set up a base camp about a mile north of the burn's boundary, near Ouzel Lake (an appropriate spot, since Rich's favorite species of bird is the ouzel, or dipper). We place our tent about two hundred feet from the granite ledge on which we cook, find an overhanging cliff face from which we can suspend our food and garbage, filter a few quarts of water, and retreat from the incessant mosquitoes to our tent. The next day we set out for an appropriately named dome—Bald Knob—just north of Ouzel Lake.

The bushwhack up to the knob is just about the steepest climb I've ever made over vegetated terrain. The summit of the knob is at eleven thousand feet, and the dark gray granite is completely exposed over the top three hundred feet. At the base of the last pitch to the summit on the north side of the knob, a large snowfield has melted down about three feet from its winter depth. Where the snowfield had covered the bedrock, the granite retains its glacial polish, but above the top of the snowbank's winter accumulation the surface is noticeably weathered. The snow has protected the bedrock from repeated freeze-thaw cycles, keeping its polish intact. This is the first time I have witnessed protection from weathering offered by a late-season snowfield. The snowfield also restricted any lichen growth on the granite. But above the snow line the gray granite is almost black, thickly carpeted with dark crustose lichens. A smattering of green map lichen looks more vibrant than usual, being set off by the surrounding sea of black.

From the top of the knob we can see Granite Peak—Montana's highest summit—to the north. Its neighboring peaks, with names such as Froze to Death Mountain, Tempest, and Storm, suggest that this is a place where the elements are severe. I can also clearly see a line at about eleven thousand feet where green alpine meadows start to be replaced by bare, weathered gray substrates. At that elevation snow doesn't melt out until late in summer, which means the growing season is too short to support lush alpine vegetation.

Scattered all around Bald Knob are lakes of various sizes. Unlike the linearly arranged tarns found in the Wind Rivers' glacial staircase valleys, these lakes lie everywhere. What I see is a landscape that was completely covered by glacial ice, with only the highest peaks emerging like islands. Ouzel Lake is the second to last tarn in a glacial valley, but I can see another dozen lakes scattered above the valley between ten and eleven thousand feet. The lakes region to the northwest of Bald Knob seems to have the most exposed domes. These will be the focus of my explorations tomorrow.

On our descent from Bald Knob we can look directly down into the clear waters of the tarn above Ouzel Lake. It's easy to see groups of large trout slowly circling the perimeter of the lake. Everyone we encounter on the trails has come to this section of the mountains to fish, and seeing the trout in those glorious alpine lakes further convinces me that a fly-rod will be essential equipment for a future outing to the Beartooths.

The next day Rich and I part company after lunch so I can explore the complex of domes I saw from Bald Knob. The geological, human, and natural histories of the Wind Rivers and Beartooths are so similar that they could easily be combined in a single chapter of this book. But on this day I experience what differentiates the granite domes of the two ranges.

THE ALPINE BLOOM

At an elevation of about ten thousand feet, between Twin and Basin Lakes, numerous small exposed domes rise above lush alpine meadows. It is this unique combination of domes, meadows, and lakes that characterizes the Beartooths. Where domes occur in the Wind Rivers, the terrain is either too rugged or too dry to support lush alpine meadows. But in the Beartooths the granite has weathered into deeper, finer-grained substrates, making extensive meadows common. The region also receives far more moisture. It isn't just the large snow-fields, still melting back in late July, that signal this, but the lush, wet-sited flora as well. My plant list shows twice as many alpine species occurring in the Beartooths as in the Wind Rivers. The most striking assemblages are found either in granite crevice communities or in wet meadows situated below receding snowfields.

One of the first crevice communities I encounter near Basin Lake stops me in my tracks. Here, surrounded by exposed granite, is a crevice filled with mountain marsh marigold, its pure white blooms looking like the flowers of an anemone and its robust fleshy leaves like a head of Bibb lettuce. As its name suggests, this is a species found in saturated substrates. Such a broad-leaved, large-flowered plant seems out of place dominating a crevice. Where is the water coming from to support this wet-sited species? Farther up the dome I see a snowbank whose meltwater trickles over the granite and, beyond a large glacial boulder, irrigates the crevice that pitches down toward the marigolds. I remember the moist depression communities in the Wind Rivers and how astounded I was by the profusion of elephant head, violet, and pink mountain heather. But this lush crevice community completely alters my frame of reference.

A bit farther up the dome I come upon another crevice filled with western spring beauty. This wet-sited wildflower is usually found below late-lying snowfields. The spring beauty deserves its name, but to fully appreciate it I need to bend down to greet it. The white flower has five petals graced with delicate pink to bright red lines. When I stand above these flowers the lines on the petals are hard to distinguish, but on bent knee their bold pattern stands out, changing a fine little flower into an exquisite beauty. What is most amazing about its presence in the crevice is that this species has marble-sized corms, similar to small potatoes. In fact, when cooked the tubers taste like potatoes. This is the only time I've seen a tuberous-rooted plant growing in a crevice on exposed granite; usually crevice plants have extensive, fibrous root systems that efficiently extract nutrients and moisture, not bulbous roots like the spring beauty's. The white flowers cut a stripe through the dark gray, lichen-covered bedrock, making the spring beauties resemble star clusters in the arm of a galaxy. These two crevice communities thoroughly challenge my previous notions about the *xeric* nature of granite balds.

Above the snowfield that waters the marsh marigolds and spring beauties, the crevice communities are more typical of those found on granite. In these drier sites alpine pussytoes often dominates, creating dense mats of woolly gray leaves. Dominance is not uncommon for this species, which can reproduce vegetatively through *stolons* (creeping stems that root and produce new plants). As another intriguing reproductive strategy, the flowers of alpine pussytoes don't need to be pollinated in order to produce viable seeds. This species' ability to clone has produced numerous genetically isolated races, making its taxonomy exceedingly complex.

Often associated with the pussytoes in the drier crevices are spotted saxifrage and roseroot. The spotted saxifrage is named for the purple, orange, and yellow spots that dot its tiny white petals. Like the pussytoes, it forms dense mats. The roseroot is an old favorite of mine. This little sedum produces an inflorescence that looks like a miniature, rose-red floret of broccoli. These three species look dramatically different from the leafy green marigolds and spring beauties. Being adapted to dry conditions, the pussytoes and saxifrage have tiny basal leaves covered in wool to prevent desiccation. The roseroot is a *succulent,* a plant with fleshy tissue that stores water for times of drought. It is an exciting find—such different crevice communities less than a hundred meters apart on the same dome!

Near the dome's top is a glacial erratic—a black basalt boulder that stands out dramatically against the lighter granite. The north side of the boulder is covered with a maze of light green, produced by the outward growth of a target lichen's concentric rings. Here, more than two thousand miles west and more than a mile higher in elevation, is the same lichen

A wind-stunted limber pine

commonly found on granite domes near my home. The realization is comforting—I am in a new environment with an old friend.

Close to the erratic is one of the most wind-stunted limber pines I have ever seen. It creeps a distance of fifteen feet over the granite, never rising more than one foot in height. On this still afternoon it is hard to imagine the winter winds that have for centuries pruned and deformed the ancient pine. To the southeast of the pine, some of the granite has been quarried, creating a wall that drops two feet. Tucked against the wall's base is a large crevice community dominated by a mixture of creeping juniper, dwarf blueberry, and arctic willow. All are dry-sited shrubs that need protection from winter desiccation. Although no snow is present, I can imagine a snowbank—two feet deep—providing protection for these alpine shrubs.

I decide to head to the next bald to the south and during my descent come upon a small slope of talus. Some of the rocks have a mantle of bright orange caloplaca—a foliose lichen that in the Rockies suggests the presence of pikas (small, short-eared relatives of rabbits). Pikas often live in talus slopes, where cavities among the boulders provide good sites for an animal to store its winter food supply—miniature mounds of hay harvested during summer. The pika usually has a number of sentinel posts on larger boulders where it sunbathes, gives its loud, single-noted call, and watches for predators. Spending a lot of time on these boulders, the pika urinates on them frequently. Caloplaca happens to be a species of lichen that can't fix nitrogen. It thus thrives on the sentinel posts, where it receives ample nitrogen from the pika's urine. Knowing this, it's easy to get a face-to-face look at this cute alpine mammal: Simply sit quietly next to a bright orange, lichen-covered sentinel post. Usually within five minutes a curious pika will climb up to see if the intruder has departed.

Between some of the talus boulders are pockets of soil, and in these, clumps of yellow columbine and snow cinquefoil look as if they have been planted to grace the pika's abode. Having long spurs that hold nectar, columbine has co-evolved with long-tongued pollinators

such as hummingbirds and butterflies. Since hummingbirds are attracted to bright reds, it's a good bet that butterflies pollinate the yellow columbine. The snow cinquefoil has very woolly leaves, much like the alpine pussytoes—a strategy that protects it from desiccation and ultraviolet radiation at these high altitudes by reflecting light and shading the leaf's surface.

At the base of the talus slope is an ample snowfield and below that a glorious wet meadow in full summer bloom. Here I encounter not only dense concentrations of mountain marsh marigold and western spring beauty but also an array of new species, including both pink and yellow mountain heather, elephant head, globeflower, rosy paintbrush, and the few-flowered shooting star. This last species, having only two or three small blooms at any one time, makes up in quality what it lacks in quantity, with possibly the most stunning of all alpine displays. The shooting star has five magenta petals fused into a corolla. Most flowers have corollas that form tubular or bell-shaped blossoms. Not the shooting star. Its flower is turned inside out so the fused petals trail behind, giving the sense that it is rocketing through space. With its brilliant petals bent back, a bright yellow-and-purple spike juts forward, supporting the anthers and stigma. The red color of this flower attracts bees, whose buzzing—vibrations produced through their high-speed wing movements when they hover—triggers the release of pollen. I have seen shooting stars too many times to count, yet every time I am compelled to stop and admire their breathtaking flowers.

Of all the granite domes I've visited, these are the richest in terms of alpine wildflowers. They are also smaller in stature than most domes, rising only one or two hundred feet above their alpine meadows. Together these features create a softer and far more intimate landscape than found among the Wind River domes. For the rest of the afternoon I stride over granite, across snowfields, past lakeshores, and through flower-filled alpine meadows. The only evidence that this paradise could experience harsh conditions is the severely wind-contorted limber pines. Here at the close of July, the austerity I often associate with granite domes is veiled under blankets of wildflowers.

Domes of the Enchantment Basin backed by Little Annapurna

CHAPTER NINE

The Enchantments:
Land of Contrasts

Names such as *Snow Creek* and *Icicle Creek* give the impression of a cold landscape with icy watersheds, but as we get out of the truck at the junction of these two drainages, it is sunny, still, and hot. Soon we will don seventy-five-pound packs, begin a ten-mile hike, and climb more than a vertical mile of relief. To make matters worse, the first half mile of the trail ascends seven hundred feet of steep south-facing slope laid bare of its ponderosa pine forest by a recent fire, and it is noon. As we organize our gear, no one mentions the hot work that lies ahead. In my mind I am already closing in on the end of the trail and what we will find in this legendary region of the Cascades—the Enchantment Lakes and their guardian peaks, the Cashmere Crags.

For this excursion I have the company of my good friends Deb Frey and Eric Love. Both Deb and Eric work for the Trust for Public Land in Santa Fe and are taking some vacation time to explore this part of the Cascades. Avid climbers, Eric and Deb have come prepared for technical ascents on both rock and snow. The climbing gear adds weight, but they are strategic in what we pack.

I've often heard that the North Cascades of Washington offer the most dramatic relief of any mountains in the continental United States. The Enchantments are part of the Stuart Range, named for the second highest nonvolcanic mountain in the state. At ninety-four hundred feet, Mount Stuart is eight thousand feet higher than our trailhead. Nowhere in the Rockies or the high Sierra is there so much vertical relief between trailhead and summit. Mount Stuart also has another distinction—it is the most massive mountain in the United States, composed solely of granite with a ridgeline more than six miles in length. If my exploration of the exposed domes that intermix with the Enchantment Lakes can be accomplished in two days, our plans leave open the option of summiting Mount Stuart, something Eric particularly wants to do. As we will eventually find out, six days isn't enough time to for us to make it to the summit of Mount Stuart—the rugged relief is all it's been said to be.

We cross Icicle Creek and quickly begin our steep climb. The weight and heat keep us to a slow but steady pace. Two miles farther we leave the burn, enter a delightfully shaded canopy of Douglas fir and western red cedar, and reach Snow Creek. After a quick dip we resume our hike and soon find ourselves climbing a glacial stairway. It is close to sunset when we reach Upper Snow Lake, the last tarn in the stairway before a steep fourteen-hundred-foot ascent to Lake Viviane, the first lake of the Enchantments. We are all ready to stop for the night, and set up camp in a mosquito swarm. We haven't seen mosquitoes all day until now, when we've reached Upper Snow Lake at fifty-four hundred feet. As in the Wind Rivers and Beartooths, mosquitoes will be constant, unwelcome companions.

The next day we make the steep climb to Lake Viviane and come to one of the most treacherous stream crossings I've experienced. About half the people with permits to enter the Enchantments elect to make this crossing with day packs only. As a result, we encounter a small village of tents clustered on the domes between Viviane and Naiad Lakes, just before the crossing. The Enchantments are a string of five major tarns and a number of lesser ones stretched out west to east, draining a snow-packed, three-square-mile basin. And all the water leaving the Enchantment Basin flows out of Lake Viviane in a rushing torrent that takes a four-hundred-foot vertical plunge about fifty feet downstream from the lake's shoreline. From previous flooding, an eighteen-inch-wide subalpine fir log spans the fifteen-foot cascade—our only means of crossing. A number of people who chose to set up camp on this side of the crossing watch us as we contemplate whether or not to cross with full packs. A misplaced footstep could mean a five-foot fall into the rushing stream and the possibility of being swept toward the falls just downstream. After a few minutes of discussion, we agree that there are enough boulders in the stream to prevent a person from making it to the falls, and with climbing ropes easily accessible we decide to attempt the crossing. Eric and Deb go first; and now it's my turn. I undo my belly strap, exhale deeply, and begin the crossing. I find myself in a debate over whether or not intense concentration is helpful—maybe if I focus too hard, my body will tense up and I'll fall? Luckily, I make it across without a mishap—thankful to be standing on a broad expanse of granite. We set up camp at seven thousand feet on a ridgetop, partially forested with subalpine fir and whitebark pine, that lies east of Leprechaun Lake. Following lunch I take cameras and journal to begin my exploration of the Enchantments.

LAND OF CONTRASTS

As I cross the outlet of Leprechaun Lake on a snowfield that stretches two hundred feet, I realize that spring is just beginning here. It's the first week of August. The previous winter set all-time records for snow accumulation in the Cascades, with Mount Baker setting a new national record of more than a hundred feet! The same winter conditions affected the Beartooths, but despite being three thousand feet lower in elevation the Enchantments have more than four times the snowpack of the Beartooths, based on the percentage of the basin that is covered in snow. This is a land of contrasts—snow and rock, white and black.

The rock of the Enchantment Basin is a medium-grained light gray granite, but the tops, north-, and south-facing sides of any granite outcrop or glacial boulder are black—covered by a dense, velvety coating of funaria. With prevailing winds from the west, the eastern sides of outcrops hold late-lying snowfields that keep the granite perfectly clean. On western sides harsh winter ice-blasting keeps funaria from establishing. The contrasts among the black funaria, the light gray exposed granite, and the ample brilliant white snowfields make me think of an Ansel Adams print. On the tops of exposed domes funaria covers 95 percent of the bedrock and easily outcompetes the common foliose lichen, black rock tripe.

Of all the granites covered in this book, the Stuart batholith is at ninety million years the youngest; it was created by subduction of the Farallon Plate beneath the North American Plate at that time. Yet in places its granite is so completely encrusted by funaria and rock tripe that it looks more ancient than the granites in the Rockies, which are ten to twenty times older. These granite domes are also the most barren of any I've visited. Not only are funaria and black rock tripe the sole colonizers of the exposed granite, but the crevice communities also support few species.

The granite has few vertical joints, although glacial quarrying has created a number of broad north–south catchments that are filled with sand. Other than some species of sedges and rushes—plants that die back to roots at the end of the growing season—all the plants in the crevice communities are evergreen *microphylls* (meaning "small leaved"). The four most common species are narrowleaf stonecrop, Tolmie's saxifrage (whose basal leaves look amazingly like sedum), pink mountain heather, and bell mountain heather. In a place with such short growing seasons (due to extended snow cover), being an evergreen makes good sense: These plants can begin photosynthesis as soon as the snow melts without having to wait until they grow new leaves. Since summers are dry on this eastern side of the Cascades— where more than 90 percent of the eighty inches of annual precipitation comes as snow, having microphyllus leaves also helps prevent desiccation during the growing season.

More than 50 percent of the catchments that I encounter hold mostly unvegetated, exposed sands. There are two possible explanations for this: either the snowbanks that filled these catchments melted out too late, restricting all plant growth, or frequent disturbance by mountain goats keeps them free of vegetation. Since I commonly find large crevice communities with patches of vegetation here and there, which don't seem to be the result of differing amounts of snow deposition, mountain goats appear to be responsible for the open crevice communities. I've read about the Enchantments' mountain goats, but I'm truly not prepared for my first encounter with them, which will happen tomorrow.

PEOPLE AND GOATS

Deb, Eric, and I are hiking about a mile from camp to the northwest of Lake Viviane. We part company so I can explore the domes in that area; Eric and Deb continue on to climb the six-hundred-foot spire of Prusik Peak. Five minutes later I need to relieve myself. We have been told to urinate only on bedrock, never on soil or vegetation. I soon experience firsthand the reason for doing so. I don't know if I'm being watched or if the sound of my stream attracts them, but within a minute a herd of about two dozen mountain goats—all females and juveniles—race to where I was standing and butt each other for an opportunity to lick my urine. Urine left on soil or vegetation virtually guarantees that the goats will eat the plants, but on exposed bedrock little damage is done.

I'm amazed by the bold activity of all the goats and fail to notice two juveniles standing directly behind me. Feeling a raspy tongue on my neck, I jolt from my seated position in time to see both young goats spring four vertical feet. It's apparent that all three of us feel similar levels of adrenaline. It seems clear that the goats are not only salt deprived but well accustomed to the presence of people, too. Certainly this is a result of the popularity of the Enchantments and the densities of campers that existed for decades prior to the issuing of permits by lottery.

The number of mountain goats in the vicinity of our camp is unusually high. I'm convinced this is the reason for the unvegetated crevice communities: The grazing pressure is simply too great. The goats also prefer the wind-protected, sand-filled depressions as bedding sites. During the next couple of days I come upon numerous round depressions in the crevice communities' exposed sands—sites where goats spent the night. Usually humans are the

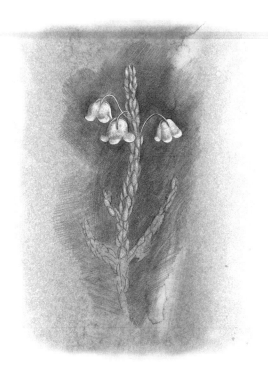

Bell mountain heather

direct cause of loss of vegetation in mountainous areas exposed to heavy traffic. But here in the Enchantments goats attracted to the garbage and urine of people have overpopulated and degraded the ecosystem.

These female mountain goats are the most morose-looking critters I have ever seen. They move slowly (unless they're fighting over urine), heads bent downward with expressionless eyes. Their maternal instincts seem to have left them. Mothers don't think twice about butting one of their young away from a urine lick and have no interest in nursing their newborns. Their blank eyes remind me of those I've seen in pictures of people suffering starvation. I wonder if the very late season and huge amounts of snow cover, on top of an already limited food supply, have resulted in the whole herd being undernourished. If so, there will be a lot of juvenile mortality come winter.

The two plants that blanket most of the vegetated crevice communities, as well as the understories of the conifer forests, are the pink and bell mountain heathers. I assume that their significant presence means the goats don't browse them. Each is covered with blooms, creating swaths of pink and white scattered here and there in forest canopy gaps or on the granite itself. No rock gardener could create more beautiful arrangements. The bell mountain heather is also called moss plant—named for its tiny evergreen leaves, the smallest to be found on any woody plant in North America. To see exquisite bell-shaped white flowers on top of stems that resemble the most delicate of mosses is a real treat—one I never tire of.

I've mentioned that the Enchantment Basin is a land of contrasts. This is best illustrated in the granite itself. The lakes wind around graceful round domes that rise in steps to about seventy-four hundred feet, creating a seemingly soft and supple landscape. Then the steep walls of the basin jut another thousand vertical feet above the domes into the most amazing arêtes I've ever seen. These form what are called the Cashmere Crags—ridgelines and summits consisting of dozens of sheer, sharp granite spires that look more dramatic than a row of teeth in a shark's mouth. Rounded domes sheltering beautiful lakes and surrounded by a stockade of granite spires make the Enchantment Basin feel like Shangri-la—a place worthy of protection.

The first person to write about the Enchantment Basin was a geology professor, Israel Russel, in 1897. Climbing to the ridgeline of Mount McCellan, he looked into the Enchantment Basin and described it as "a great cathedral-like mass of clustering spires rising within an amphitheater." But the Enchantments would remain virtually unknown for another half century, until rugged climbers started conquering their spires. Two intrepid explorers, Bill and Peg Stark, gave the Enchantment Lakes and the Cashmere Crags many of their mythical names, conjuring images of lost legendary landscapes. It was the magical nature of the area, with its pristine lakes and domes surrounded by the fortress walls, that inspired such names as Rune Lake, Talisman Lake, Leprechaun Lake, Brynhild Lake, Gnome Tarn; and arêtes such as Dragontail, the Black Dwarves, and the Nightmare Needles.

Eric and Deb have direct experience with some of these dramatic spires, but my closest encounter with the Cashmere Crags came with the ascent of eighty-four-hundred-foot Little Annapurna, which frames the basin's southwest side. This is the only mountain in the Enchantments that doesn't require a technical climb to reach its summit. But since I am without ice ax and crampons, we rope up for the ascent over one section of Snow Creek Glacier. Just one hundred years ago this glacier covered more than a square mile—almost the

An Enchantment dome backed by the rugged spires of
the Cashmere Crags

entire upper basin above seventy-four hundred feet. Today the glacier has receded into five sections that cover less than a quarter of that area.

We stop to eat lunch at one of the glacier's recessional moraines. Scattered about the moraine's base are a number of alpine plants that were absent from the domes and lakeshores I'd been exploring the past three days. Since the upper basin has 90 percent snow cover, I guess that the mountain goats rarely venture up here, allowing these species to survive. Rosy paintbrush, white alpine phlox, pink monkey flower, and yellow Martindale's lomatium add color to this otherwise gray-and-white landscape. The lomatium is a member of the parsley family and looks and smells just like the garden herb—a strong fragrance in a place otherwise devoid of odors.

After lunch we rope up and make the summit as a thunderstorm approaches from the west. The summit is a flat fellfield about one hundred meters broad. We cut southwest across the summit to a rocky promontory and look over the edge into Crystal Creek ravine. The view is staggering; it catches even Eric and Deb by surprise. We are looking straight down more than three thousand feet. The earth has literally fallen away on this side of the ridge—a confirmation of the nature of vertical relief in the Cascades. Across the ravine stand the Nightmare Needles—a most intricate jumble of spires. All told there must be two dozen spires capping an arête less than a mile in length. We are compelled to stare into the abyss of this deep glacial ravine even as lightning strikes McCellen Peak, less than two miles away. But the resulting "thunder boomer," as Deb and Eric like to call them, breaks our gaze and we make a hasty retreat from the summit.

It's as if the Cashmere Crags magically protect the basin and forbid the thunderstorm entry. We can hear distant thunder during our descent, but not one lightning strike hits the rim of the basin, and only a gentle rain falls on the snow, lakes, and granite—quite different from a Rocky Mountain thunderstorm. As we work our way between Talisman and Rune Lakes, it becomes clear just how late the summer season is this year. It's August 7 and at seventy-one hundred feet, Talisman Lake is completely iced over. We wind our way along lakeshores, across snowfields, up and over marvelous domes experiencing the rain and glowing mats of heather. We walk through groves of trees and come upon a remarkable whitebark pine. This species is ecologically similar to the limber pine found in the Rockies, and like limber pine grows to great age in exposed alpine sites. The tree before us must be at least a thousand years old.

It grows in an exposed sand depression to a height of four feet, where its top just crests the surrounding granite. Its canopy then splays out flat for a distance of six feet. Despite its lack of height, this tree's trunk is two and a half feet in diameter, giving it the appearance of a stout short toadstool! I'm guessing the pine hasn't changed much in centuries and probably had a similar stature at the time of Columbus's voyage. But of all the trees in the basin, the alpine larch most catches my attention.

I've always had a special attraction to larch. After the yellow, orange, and red autumn leaves of birch, aspen, and maple fall in New England, out comes the glorious turning foliage of the larch—a color Aldo Leopold called "smoky gold." Larches are the only deciduous conifers in North America (an adaptation for retaining moisture in extremely cold, dry climates), and the quality of light under their delicate golden canopies as their foliage prepares to drop is heavenly. I can only imagine what open groves of alpine larch would look like growing around the lakes and silhouetted against the Enchantment domes come fall—their smoky gold backed by gray granite and reflected in lakes of blue. This year their growing season will be short, for many trees on northern exposures are just breaking bud in this first week in August, and leaf fall will commence in two months. With growing seasons this short, the larches, which rarely grow to more than two feet in diameter, are far older than they appear.

The larch's ability to drop its leaves allows the tree to grow in sites where other conifers— subalpine fir and whitebark pine—can't venture. Larch doesn't need to be tucked into wind-protected microenvironments; it easily grows right on top of the domes, exposed to the full

Alpine larch

force of winter winds. Obviously, because the tree drops its leaves, ice-blasting does not significantly affect its survival. Yet exposed larches often grow as spindly spires, with undulating trunks reminiscent of the cedars in a Van Gogh painting. One grove of skinny, wavy, younger alpine larches, on the northern shore of Rune Lake, could be an illustration from a Dr. Seuss book. The larches only accentuate the magical nature of the Enchantments.

Although the domes in this basin host far less biotic diversity than any other granite balds that I've explored, they're extremely compelling. Their beauty lies in the stark contrasts between lakes, snow, and black-encrusted granite, graced with blooming heaths and delicate larch and backed by a fortress of spires. It's no wonder that the rugged ascent into this basin has not been a deterrent to thousands of climbers and hikers. I know this is a place I will return to in a few years, when I will have the time to watch the smoky gold of larch add its heavenly glow to the domes and lakes of the Enchantment Basin.

Looking west over Tenaya Lake, Yosemite National Park

CHAPTER TEN

Yosemite: Range of Light

"Above all others the range of light" is John Muir's singular description of the Sierra Nevada of California. I contemplate this quote as I drive to the trailhead that will take me to Golden Trout Camp on the edge of the John Muir Wilderness. Why should the Sierra be more a range of light than the Rockies? This section of the eastern Sierra supplies the answer. It's a dry, open landscape with granite eroding into deep, white, gravelly sands. On hikes out of Golden Trout Camp, through the subalpine, and on into the alpine, the quality of light is extraordinary, especially at sunrise and sunset. Here and there thousand-year-old lodgepole and foxtail pines stand as sentinels above the white substrate—the deeply fissured bark of their trunks glowing a brilliant orange red. Muir was right.

In summer, when only 5 percent of the region's precipitation falls, these high peaks are bathed in rarefied sunlight. In contrast, the Rockies receive a good portion of their annual precipitation during the summer thunderstorms that frequent their high peaks. Out of the two weeks I spend in the Sierra during August 2000, I will experience only one light rainfall. A week later, during my exploration of Yosemite National Park, Muir's words will echo time and again, and not once will I find them out of place.

I enter Yosemite from the east via Tioga Pass. My first order of business is to locate my friends Chris Papouchis and Andrew Stemple. I missed my rendezvous with them yesterday due to car trouble. So I head to the store at Tuolumne Meadows and easily find their note instructing me to meet them at the parking lot adjacent to Lembert Dome. As I pull in, they look relieved that I have made it and in celebration decide to forgo organizing our backpacks. Instead, they lead me directly to the base of Lembert and suggest that we not waste any time before grounding ourselves on a classic Yosemite dome.

Like many of Yosemite's domes, Lembert is steep sided. No talus lies on its southern flanks, telling me that this side of the dome has been stable, with no exfoliation, since the glacial ice departed this valley ten thousand years ago. The extensive glacial polish on Lembert's surface confirms this fact. Compared to the domes I've been exploring in the Rockies and Cascades, Lembert is decidedly different. This granite is completely unjointed for hundreds of meters and covered with glacial polish. As a result, the bedrock supports almost no vegetation. Every so often we encounter a bonsai-like whitebark pine growing in a small crevice, but this is basically all we see. On this steep, southern face there are no crevice communities—nothing but a smattering of black crustose lichen until we reach the dome's more level top. Ice creep has done its job in keeping almost all plant life at bay.

As we work our way up the steep, smooth bedrock, other domes of white granite begin to stand out in the distance. Some rise directly above meadows, looking oddly out of place, like white monuments meant for Washington, D.C. We're surrounded by glowing green shades of forest, meadow, marsh, and white glaciated granite. Muir's words return to me; yes, this is the range of light.

On many of Yosemite's domes more than 95 percent of the granite remains free of vegetation other than some cyanobacteria or crustose lichens. What would make these domes so different from all the others I've visited in our northern states? The secret to the granite of these domes is that it is fine grained and, even more important, lacks vertical joints, creating the most glorious unvegetated expanses of granite found anywhere in the United States.

Upon reaching the top of Lembert, we decide to look for a gentler means of descent, but the northern and western sides are more than sixty degrees in pitch, ruling out any nontechnical down climb. So we retrace our steps on the south side. I am impressed by Andrew's and Chris's surefootedness. With certain areas reaching a forty-five-degree pitch, I don't have faith in the friction-holding capacity of my boots and have to crab-walk these sections while my friends are able to remain standing. A loss of footing on this dome would be serious. With nothing but smooth granite for hundreds of feet below, arresting a fall would be impossible.

With care and concentration we make it back to the parking area, organize our gear, and head to a trailhead on the north side of Tenaya Lake. To avoid the crowds that cluster around Route 120 and still sample a diversity of domes, Andrew's plan is to explore the region that frames the northern watershed of the lake and then head into the Grand Canyon of the Tuolumne River below Glen Aulin. Our hike begins in a dense forest of red fir and lodgepole pine, but about a mile up the trail we encounter an extensive slab of granite — larger than a football field — that gently sweeps up to the east. Occasional flooding has kept the bedrock free of vegetation other than scattered tree islands. Numerous glacial boulders grace its surface, giving it three-dimensional depth and creating a landscape reminiscent of Salvador Dali. Not wanting to hold up our hike, I decide to return to this spot the next day. About four miles down the trail we bushwhack a mile to the east, set up camp, and then in the early evening set out to explore Polly Dome — the most vegetatively diverse bald we'll encounter.

As we approach Polly Dome we hike through more red fir forest, and where granite ledge breaks the forest floor we begin to encounter glorious specimens of western white pine with basal diameters of up to four feet. These trees are strikingly reminiscent of the eastern white

Glacial boulder field

pine found in New England, growing as straight, tall columns that rise above the rest of the red fir canopy. The understory of the red fir forests is also familiar. Nothing grows under their dense canopies, a feature common under the deep shade of eastern hemlock in New England. Ten feet above the ground the branches and trunks of the fir support almost iridescent, chartreuse clumps of the fruiticose lichen letharia. The height of the lichen line indicates persistent winter snow cover. The red fir forest is also called the snow forest, since it occupies the elevational zone that receives the most snowfall in the Sierra—up to forty feet a year. Both late-lying snow and dense shade create somber fir monocultures with no other trees, shrubs, or herbaceous plants.

We leave the deep shade of the forest and ascend the lower ledges of Polly Dome. The granite here is quite different from that on Lembert. It is coarser grained with large, well-formed hornblende crystals and huge feldspar *phenocrysts* (crystals much larger than all the others minerals in a rock). Many of these phenocrysts are greater than three inches in length and rise above the granite's surface, displaying their resistance to erosion. I can't help but think what fine finger- and toeholds these large feldspar crystals offer to climbers. The lower portions of this side of Polly Dome form a staircase of exposed ledges, with each shelf rising fifteen to twenty feet. As we climb, each shelf we come upon supports new plant communities.

The first shelf contains pockets of haircap moss being invaded by pussypaws, with dense gray basal rosettes and delicate pink flower tufts. Like alpine pussytoes in the Rockies, the leaves of these pussypaws are covered with fine hair to protect them from summer desiccation and damage from ultraviolet radiation. Tucked against the back of the shelf is a bank of pinemat manzanita—its lustrous, red-barked branches creeping over the granite. Pinemat fills the same niche on exposed granite as bearberry (to which it is closely related) in the East, causing me to flash back to similar granite shelves in Acadia National Park. But here the view does not encompass ocean; it overlooks dark green forests from which white domes rise like smooth lenticular clouds.

Continuing our ascent, we begin to pick up the faint aromatic odor of mountain penny-royal, which strengthens dramatically as we climb through beds where it has colonized small aprons of scree that lead from one shelf to the next. Sometimes called coyote or mustang mint, pennyroyal's smell is actually more reminiscent of pungent sage than of the mint family to which it belongs. Its cleansing fragrance is a wonderful addition to the otherwise unscented air normally experienced on granite domes. Pennyroyal's flower head doesn't look like much from a distance, but close inspection reveals tiny purple flowers that are exquisite in design and coloration.

The higher we climb, the more variety we encounter. Showy flowers such as cream-colored Leichtlin's mariposa lily, scarlet Indian paintbrush, rose-red mountain pride, orange-red California fuchsia, pink fireweed, and pink mountain heather abound in crevice communities established on the granite steps. The large percentage of tubular red flowers suggests the importance of hummingbirds as pollinators, but we don't see or hear any in our vicinity.

The granite ledges are covered with colorful lichens as well—black, slate gray, dark gray, rich brown, and yellow orange. Funaria moss is also common on these vegetated ledges, which are free of disturbance by ice creep. With their ample vegetation, the lower sections of Polly Dome are a botanist's delight—the antithesis of Lembert's steeper, ice-scoured granite.

Ice creep may not affect these ledges, but fire does. We come upon a broad shelf covered with fireweed and young lodgepole seedlings, each supporting five whorls of branches that date the fire to half a decade before our exploration. The fire was restricted to this shelf. We are more than a mile from the nearest trail, and this has been a rigorous bushwhack. Would other people have ventured to this partially forested dome and started an accidental fire here, or was it the result of lightning? I would guess lightning, since hikers are usually drawn to more exposed domes. Polly Dome continues to climb in ever-increasing steps, and we are only about halfway to the top. With evening well on its way, Chris, Andrew, and I decide it is

Hanging gardens of pinemat manzanita

time to head back to camp. This first day has highlighted the diverse and dramatic nature of Yosemite's domelands.

The next morning I head off on my own to check out the domes on the western side of the drainage and to return to the site with all the glacial boulders. I bushwhack westward more than a mile from camp and begin to ascend a dome that shows signs of recent exfoliation. The dome rises in a series of steep vertical steps. The lower steps are roughly twenty feet in height, decreasing to just two feet toward the top—a classic example of thinning expansion joints. Although it is tricky finding a route up this dome, the most difficult part is traversing the huge talus slope that lies at its base. It is a hot, sunny day, and forested pockets among the talus give a brief respite from the heat. Mountain hemlock associates with lodgepole pine and red fir in these pocket forests, while alpine gooseberry spreads over the older talus beneath them.

I leave the talus and climb toward the top of the dome. Stunted and gnarled western junipers greet me—their brilliant rusty red bark resembling flames spouting from the light bedrock. Associated with the juniper are beds of pinemat that cover level granite shelves and then cascade over their lips, creating dark green hanging gardens. The combination of the scattered juniper and opulent beds of pinemat conjures up a steep, terraced Mediterranean hillside. At six hundred feet above the valley floor, I can see for miles in all directions with no sign of other people, even though I know that just three miles distant the Tenaya Lake area is overcrowded. I have this entire glorious dome to myself and spend the rest of the day sitting, leisurely strolling, and exploring every shelf the bald offers. I can't imagine a better way to spend a Yosemite afternoon.

On the dome's top, where crevices aren't covered by pinemat, selaginella (a type of spike moss) appears to be the pioneer, followed by pussypaws and Wright's eriogonum (one of the Sierra's many endemic species of buckwheat). They are then colonized by sedges or commonly by California fuchsia. It's intriguing that a large-flowered plant like the fuchsia can colonize such a dry, wind-exposed site as a crevice on the top of a Yosemite dome. In the driest of crevices narrowleaf stonecrop often forms pure stands of tightly packed rosettes looking like miniature clumps of bananas. And as always, wind-contorted whitebark pines dot the exposed granite, but it is the arrangements of juniper and pinemat that keep me on this unnamed dome for the entire afternoon.

GRAND CANYON OF THE TUOLUMNE

The next day we pack up, hike into the Grand Canyon of the Tuolumne River, and camp a bit more than a mile south of Glen Aulin on a rounded outcrop of granite, graced by a neighboring waterfall and a wonderful swimming hole. When we aren't hiking, Andrew, Chris, and I spend many hours seated on smooth granite by our poolside, sunning, having fine discussions and refreshing swims. At night we lay out our sleeping bags on level granite and watch the stars revolve above steep glacially scoured walls until the moon rises, lighting up the entire canyon like a great beacon. And even though it is mid-August in the most visited of our national parks, only once during our three-day stay does anyone venture into our site, other than a pine marten that crosses the river on a log lying over our pool's outflow.

Both sides of the canyon are lined by a phalanx of steep rounded domes rising at least a thousand feet above the river. My first exploration is on the north side of the canyon—a wonderful composite of balds and stately groves of immense western juniper. A number of

A crevice community of narrowleaf stonecrop

the junipers reach basal diameters of seven feet — much larger than I imagine this species can grow. I am staggered by their size on these seemingly harsh granite outcrops and wonder how old they are. The juniper trunks show signs of fire, having basal scars on their uphill sides where fuel pockets composed of branches and needles accumulated. Greenleaf manzanita creates abundant thigh-high thickets all around the junipers, and brilliant letharia lichen lights up the juniper's reddish branches. The contrast between the iridescent green lichen and the rich red bark of the juniper is stunning. Here and there elderberries stand above the manzanita, easily picked out by their hanging clusters of brilliant red fruits. Associated with the juniper are scattered Jeffrey pines. This close relative of ponderosa pine is found in drier and higher-elevation sites. These two pines are difficult to distinguish, but at nine thousand feet I know I am too high for the ponderosa. Later, Jeffrey pines are easily confirmed by the large, ten-inch-long cones that lie on the ground (the cones of the ponderosa rarely reach lengths of more than five inches).

As I work my way up through the grove of juniper and pine, I crest a dramatic slab of glacially polished and striated granite. As in the Rockies, everything I can see, with the exception of the highest horns in the Cathedral Range (which rise above ten thousand feet), was once covered in glacial ice. From the amount of striation, I gather that this granite is softer than most other granites. Striations are quite rare in eastern granites, but in Yosemite they are common, along with large expanses of polish.

YOSEMITE HISTORY

At 150 million years of age, this granite is young compared to that in the Rockies. It was formed by subduction of the Pacific Plate when the North American Plate began to slide westward at greater speed following the breakup of Pangaea. At that time a huge range of mountains, the ancestral Sierra, framed the western side of the continent. But erosion had reduced these mountains to a flat plain of granite when the ancestral Rockies made their rise seventy million years ago.

The Sierra Nevada we see today began its *orogeny* (a period of mountain building) about ten million years ago, with the bulk of that uplift happening in the past three million years—again, all the result of subduction. The Sierra is a tilted fault block, analogous to a hinged trapdoor that is ajar. The Sierra's western flank gradually rises like the slope of the trapdoor to its precipitous eastern escarpment. More than three million years ago gentle streams ran down its western face. But then dramatic uplift opened the trapdoor farther, creating mountains that captured more precipitation, and the streams became deep-cutting rivers. With the onset of the Pleistocene glaciations two million years ago, the river drainages were carved out into dramatic glacial valleys. The Grand Canyon of the Toulumne is one of them, but not as well known as its sister—Yosemite Valley—which is arguably the most striking geological wonder in the United States.

The first person to figure out that ice had carved the valleys and mountainous landscape of Yosemite was John Muir. During his first year in Yosemite Valley, Muir described its formation. "Nature chose for tool not the earthquake or lightning to rent and split asunder, not the stormy torrent or eroding rain, but the tender snow-flowers noiselessly falling through unnumbered centuries . . ." It's intriguing that Muir, who wasn't a geologist, was the first to propose that glaciation was the force behind the landscape he saw. The eminent geologists Josiah Dwight Whitney and William P. Blake completely missed the role of ice, respectively explaining Yosemite Valley's origin by faulting and river erosion. But it is not surprising that Muir got it right. He was a man of uncommon intellect and keen observing eye. Upon first meeting Muir in 1870, the preeminent geologist Joseph Le Conte described him as a man "of rare intelligence, of much knowledge of science, particularly of biology, of which he has made a specialty."

The human history of Yosemite Valley is every bit as dramatic as its geological history. Prior to 1851 the valley was a Shangri-la—a realm known only to a Miwok tribe named the Ahwahneechee. Their name is translated as "the people of the place of the big mouth," their name for Yosemite Valley. With the gold rush, conflict between Native peoples of the Sierra and white settlers escalated. Most tribes were forced into signing treaties that took away their lands, but—protected by their valley fortress—the Ahwahneechee remained free of contact with whites. Rumors started to surface of a tribe existing in a hidden valley to the west of San Francisco. The Mariposa Battalion, a volunteer militia formed to subdue Native tribes, was sent out to find the secret valley and remove the Ahwahneechee. The battalion encountered the valley on March 27, 1851—the first time non-Native people had set foot in it. By 1855 all the Ahwahneechee were removed, and tourists made their first excursion into Yosemite Valley. Just eight years after its 1851 discovery, C. L. Weed would take the first photographs of the valley's geological wonders, and by 1864 Abraham Lincoln would sign the Yosemite Grant giving the valley protected status eight years before the establishment of Yellowstone, the country's first national park. It's hard to believe that a place could change from tribal homeland to photographed tourist attraction in just eight years.

Through the passionate lobbying of Muir, Yosemite received national park status in 1890. At that time Basque sheepherders grazed flocks in Tuolumne Meadows and the rest of the Tuolumne River drainage. The sheep, referred to by Muir as "hooved locusts," dramatically degraded the areas they grazed, so the U.S. Cavalry patrolled the park to curtail sheep grazing until 1914, when the Basques were finally forced out.

From where I sit above the river valley, large expanses of open lodgepole pine forest with thick stands of understory grasses are visible. Less than a hundred years ago these grassy understories would have been absent, grazed down by sheep. It was Muir's advocacy of the removal of the sheep that let this valley recover, or at least this section of the valley.

Fifteen miles downstream Muir suffered his biggest loss—the damming of the Tuolumne River and the flooding of the Hetch Hetchy Valley to create a reservoir for San Francisco. Muir considered the Hetch Hetchy to be an equal to Yosemite Valley. That such a dramatic feature could be ruined within this national park was a painful blow to Muir, one that many think brought on his death within a year of the commencement of the dam's construction.

As I sit, I wonder how many times my wanderings have crossed the path of John Muir, who roamed this landscape more than a century ago. As a strong, agile man with incredible stamina and self-reliance, Muir likely left no part of Yosemite unexplored. I can envision him with his woolen bedroll and some salt and flour heading out into his "range of light" for weeks at a time. Maybe the place where I sit, contemplating this incredible valley, lies close to a place where he once did the same. As I look out over the Grand Canyon of the Tuolumne, and farther to the south where the nunataks of the Cathedral Range stand like viperous fangs, it's easy for me to understand why Muir was so connected to this landscape. I, too, embrace his words: "How softly these rocks are adorned, and how fine and reassuring the company they keep, their feet among beautiful groves and meadows, their brows in the sky . . . bathed in floods of water, floods of light . . ."

My meditation is broken as I hear Andrew and Chris off to my right climbing the steep eastern wall of a bald that's a couple of hundred feet higher than mine. I get up and stride over wonderfully sculpted granite, eventually meeting up with them on top of a dome that rises a thousand feet above the valley. At the dome's southern end a fine arrangement of glacial boulders seems perfectly placed to enhance its aesthetic beauty.

For our last sunset, Chris, Andrew, and I hike down the canyon to explore the river and its waterfalls. It is a peaceful evening, and again we encounter no one on the trail. At Waterwheel Falls we stop so Chris can get some shots of the alpenglow reflected off the upper reaches of the canyon wall. To the west is what appears to be a cloudbank. But then we begin to smell smoke: A fire is burning farther down the valley. We wonder if we'll be enveloped in smoke during our last night, but as evening descends, cold air draining down through the canyon picks up, taking the smoke with it.

The movement of the waxing moon gives us three nights in one for our final respite. As we retire to our bags, the moon is not yet above the canyon wall, but has washed out the night sky to a deep blue. Before midnight, as light fills the canyon, I am reminded of a midwinter night with its reflective, snowy landscape. Especially by moonlight, Muir's range of light holds forth. By early morning the moon has set, stars wheel in the blackness, and the polished white granite walls faintly glow in their light.

Yosemite is undoubtedly lord when it comes to the realm of granite domes. It is no accident that more people visit this national park than all others. If Yosemite had a different geology, I'm confident it wouldn't even have national park status. As dawn breaks on our final morning, I realize that of all the granite domes in the United States, these are the last to be graced by the sun. Three hours earlier the granite summit of Cadillac Mountain in Acadia was the first place in the United States to receive the sun's warmth.

PART THREE

APPENDIXES

ERA	PERIOD	EPOCH	MILLIONS OF YEARS BP
Cenozoic	Quaternary	Holocene	
			.01
		Pleistocene	
			2
	Tertiary		
			66
Mesozoic	Cretaceous		
			144
	Jurassic		
			208
	Triassic		
			246
Paleozoic	Permian		
			286
	Carboniferous		
			360
	Devonian		
			408
	Silurian		
			438
	Ordovician		
			505
	Cambrian		
			570
Precambrian	Hadrynian		
			1,000
	Helikian		
			2,000
	Aphebian		
			2,500

Geologic Time Line

Geologic time represented in the preceding table divides the history of the Earth into eras and periods. The beginning and end of each era and period is determined by marked changes occurring worldwide in the fossil record. For example, both the Paleozoic and Mesozoic Eras end with dramatic losses in the fossil record that suggest large-scale global extinctions. In the case of the Mesozoic Era, dinosaur fossils disappear 66 million years ago, marking the end of this era.

List of Plants

NONFLOWERING PLANTS

Alpine reindeer lichen	*Cladina alpestris*
Caloplaca	*Caloplaca saxicola*
Funaria	*Funaria* spp.
Green map lichen	*Rhizocarpon geographicum*
Haircap moss	*Polytrichum juniperinum*
Lecanora	*Lecanora* spp.
Letharia	*Letharia* spp.
Lungwort	*Lobaria pulmonaria*
Reindeer lichen	*Cladina rangiferina*
Rock tripe	*Umbilicaria* spp.
Selaginella	*Selaginella* spp.
Sphagnum	*Sphagnum* spp.
Target lichen	*Arctoparmelia centrifuga*

HERBACEOUS FLOWERING PLANTS

Alpine phlox	*Phlox diffusa*
Alpine pussytoes	*Antennaria alpina*

American bistort	*Polygonum bistortoides*
Bunchberry	*Cornus canadensis*
California fuchsia	*Zauschneria californica*
Early blue violet	*Viola adunca*
Elephant head	*Pedicularis groenlandica*
Few-flowered shooting star	*Dodecatheon pulchellum*
Fireweed	*Epilobium angustifolium*
Globeflower	*Trollius laxus*
Goldenrod	*Solidago* spp.
Herb Robert	*Geranium robertianum*
Indian paintbrush	*Castilleja applegatei*
Leichtlin's mariposa lily	*Calochortus leichtlinii*
Martindale's lomatium	*Lomatium martindalei*
Mertensia	*Mertensia paniculata*
Mountain marsh marigold	*Caltha leptosepala*
Mountain pennyroyal	*Monardella odoratissima*
Mountain pride	*Penstemon newberryi*
Mullein	*Verbascum thapsus*
Narrowleaf stonecrop	*Sedum lanceolatum*
Pink monkey flower	*Mimulus lewisii*
Pussypaws	*Calyptridium umbellatum*
Red baneberry	*Actaea rubra*
Roseroot	*Sedum rosea* subsp. *integrifolium*
Rosy paintbrush	*Castilleja rhexifolia*
Snow cinquefoil	*Potentilla nivea*
Spotted saxifrage	*Saxifraga bronchialis*
Three-toothed cinquefoil	*Potentilla tridentata*

Tolmie's saxifrage	*Saxifraga tolmiei*
Wallflower	*Erysimum nivale*
Western spring beauty	*Claytonia lanceolata*
Wright's eriogonum	*Eriogonum wrightii*
Yarrow	*Achillea millefolium*
Yellow columbine	*Aquilegia flavescens*

CONIFEROUS TREES AND SHRUBS

Alpine larch	*Larix lyallii*
Creeping juniper	*Juniperus horizontalis*
Douglas fir	*Pseudotsuga menziesii*
Eastern hemlock	*Tsuga canadensis*
Eastern white pine	*Pinus strobus*
Engelmann spruce	*Picea engelmannii*
Foxtail pine	*Pinus balfouriana*
Giant sequoia	*Sequoiadendron giganteum*
Incense cedar	*Calocedrus decurrens*
Jack pine	*Pinus banksiana*
Jeffrey pine	*Pinus jeffreyi*
Limber pine	*Pinus flexilis*
Lodgepole pine	*Pinus contorta*
Mountain hemlock	*Tsuga mertensiana*
Northern white cedar	*Thuja occidentalis*
Pitch pine	*Pinus rigida*
Ponderosa pine	*Pinus ponderosa*
Red fir	*Abies magnifica*
Red pine	*Pinus resinosa*
Red spruce	*Picea rubens*

Subalpine fir	*Abies lasiocarpa*
Western juniper	*Juniperus occidentalis*
Western red cedar	*Thuja plicata*
Western white pine	*Pinus monticola*
Whitebark pine	*Pinus albicaulis*
White fir	*Abies concolor*

FLOWERING TREES AND SHRUBS

Alpine gooseberry	*Ribes lasianthum*
American beech	*Fagus grandifolia*
American mountain ash	*Sorbus americana*
Arctic willow	*Salix arctica*
Aspen	*Populus tremuloides*
Bearberry	*Arctostaphylos uva-ursi*
Bear oak	*Quercus ilicifolia*
Bell mountain heather	*Cassiope tetragona*
Black birch	*Betula lenta*
Black chokeberry	*Aronia melanocarpa*
Black crowberry	*Empetrum nigrum*
Black huckleberry	*Gaylussacia baccata*
Bog bilberry	*Vaccinium uliginosum*
Dwarf blueberry	*Vaccinium boreale*
Greenleaf manzanita	*Arctostaphylos patula*
Labrador tea	*Ledum groenlandicum*
Low-bush blueberry	*Vaccinium angustifolium*
Mesquite	*Prosopis glandulosa*
Moss campion	*Silene acaulis*
Mountain cranberry	*Vaccinium vitis-idaea*

Mountain holly	*Nemopanthus mucronatus*
Mountain huckleberry	*Vaccinium membranaceum*
Mountain laurel	*Kalmia latifolia*
Paper birch	*Betula papyrifera*
Pinemat manzanita	*Arctostaphylos nevadensis*
Pink mountain heather	*Phyllodoce empetriformis*
Red elderberry	*Sambucus microbotrys*
Red maple	*Acer rubrum*
Red oak	*Quercus rubra*
Rhodora	*Rhododendron canadense*
Shad	*Amelanchier laevis*
Sheep laurel	*Kalmia angustifolia*
Shrubby cinquefoil	*Pentaphylloides floribunda*
Striped maple	*Acer pensylvanicum*
Sugar maple	*Acer saccharum*
White ash	*Fraxinus americana*
White oak	*Quercus alba*
Wild raisin	*Viburnum cassinoides*
Yellow birch	*Betula lutea*
Yellow mountain heather	*Phyllodoce glanduliflora*

Glossary

ABIOTIC an environment with no living organisms or organic material

ABYSSAL PLAIN the flattest part of the deep ocean floor, at depths of more than four thousand meters

ADVENTITIOUS BUDS buds occurring on plant structures other than twigs

ANTHOCYANIN a reddish or purplish plant pigment that absorbs heat

ARÊTE a knife-edge ridge created when the cirques or glacial valleys of two alpine glaciers merge

BASALT a dark-colored, igneous rock that is rich in iron and magnesium and is a common component of oceanic crust and fluid lava flows

BATHOLITH an exposed bed of granite that covers at least one hundred square kilometers and formed from magma that cooled many miles below the Earth's surface

CHATTER MARKS	crescent-shaped depressions in glaciated granite created by glacial boulders being forced down into the bedrock and chipping out flakes of rock
CIRQUE	a steep-sided, bowl-shaped valley in the side of a mountain, carved by an alpine glacier
CLIMAX	Frederic Clements's concept of an old-growth ecosystem that lies at the end of a successional sequence and maintains its community composition until it is disturbed
CONTINENTAL DRIFT	Alfred Wegener's theory that continents could migrate across the globe
CRUSTOSE LICHEN	a lichen that is completely welded onto its substrate
CRYPTOBIOSIS	a process by which organisms curtail all metabolic activity for prolonged periods of time and, when conditions become appropriate, resume life
CRYPTOGAMIC CARPETS	mats of spore-producing bacteria, lichens, or moss that carpet the ground
CYANOBACTERIA	bacteria that can photosynthesize; formerly called blue-green algae
EPIPHYTES	plants such as lichens, moss, or ferns that grow on trees
ERICACEOUS	woody plants that are members of the heath family
EXFOLIATION	the process by which large slabs of bedrock break loose from cliff faces by expansion within the joints of the rock

EXPANSION JOINTS　　the curvilinear fractures that form in granite domes from the pressure release produced as overlying bedrock weathers away

FELLFIELD　　an alpine tundra ecosystem in which rocks cover more than 50 percent of the ground, the result of strong winds that blow away fine materials and restrict plant growth

FIRN　　old snow that has metamorphosed into icy granules

FOLIOSE LICHEN　　a lichen that has leaflike tissues

FRACTALS　　patterns in nature that repeat themselves as smaller or larger parts are examined: feathers, clouds, river drainages, snowflakes, and fern fronds are just some examples

FRUITICOSE LICHEN　　a lichen with erect fruiting bodies

GLACIAL ERRATIC　　a glacially transported boulder that is a different type of rock from the bedrock on which it resides

GLACIAL GROOVE　　a broad U-shaped trough in bedrock formed as a glacial boulder was dragged across its surface

GLACIAL NOTCH　　a deep U-shaped valley carved by a continental glacier

GLACIAL POLISH　　the mirror-smooth finish on bedrock that has been scoured by glaciers

GLACIAL STRIATIONS　　parallel lines carved into bedrock by small hard rocks embedded in the bottom of a glacier

HORN	a steep, sharp mountain peak formed when three or more alpine glaciers merge on the flanks of mountain's summit
HOT SPOT	a circular, isolated area where a mantle plume collides with the Earth's crust, resulting in uplift and volcanic activity
HYPSITHERMAL	the warmest time of the Earth's present interglacial period, approximately six thousand years ago
ICE CREEP	the process by which snow metamorphoses into firn and ice and, on steeply sloping bedrock, slides over the rock, scouring off vegetation
IGNEOUS ROCK	rock that cools from molten magma
LAYERING	a process by which conifer branches that touch the ground can sprout roots
MAGMA	rock that has been heated to complete melting
MANTLE	rock that is plastic in nature, lies between the Earth's crust and core, and makes up the majority of the Earth's volume; being plastic, the mantle can slowly flow
MAST YEAR	a year of prolific seed production for a species of tree
METAMORPHIC ROCK	rock exposed to enough heat and pressure to cause it to partially melt and recrystallize
MICROPHYLL	a plant that has very small leaves

MID-ATLANTIC RIDGE	an underwater ridge in the middle of the Atlantic Ocean created by a rifting zone
MUTUALISM	an interaction between individuals of different species that is mutually beneficial and necessary for the survival of at least one, or more often both, species
NUNATAK	a mountain summit that remains ice-free during glaciation and acts as a refugium for alpine species
OROGENY	mountain building
PHENOCRYSTS	crystals in igneous rock that are many times larger than the surrounding matrix
PIONEERS	the first plants to colonize a primary successional site following disturbance
PLATE TECTONICS	the geological theory that combines continental drift and seafloor spreading to explain the surficial geology of the globe
PRIMARY SUCCESSION	the changes in plant communities that follow a disturbance creating an abiotic site
RELAY FLORISTICS	a term used to describe Frederic Clements's description of the process of primary succession
RHIZINAE	microscopic fungal threads that anchor a crustose lichen to rock

RHIZOMES	surficial roots that give rise to numerous aboveground plants creating clones
RHYOLITIC MAGMA	molten rock that has a high amount of silicates and as a result is viscous, producing explosive volcanic events when it surfaces
RIFTING ZONE	a linear region on the Earth's surface where two crustal plates are being forced apart resulting in volcanic activity
ROCHE MOUTONNÉE	literally, "stone sheep," a European term that describes glaciated rock outcrops that display a gentle rise to a steep quarried face and are shaped like sheep lying in a pasture
SEAFLOOR SPREADING	Harry Hess's theory that oceanic rifting zones drive the migration of tectonic plates across the globe
SEAMOUNT	an underwater circular mountain massif generated by a hot spot
SECONDARY SUCCESSION	a series of changes in plant communities that is initiated by a disturbance that leaves organisms, or at least components of the soil, intact
SEDIMENTARY ROCK	rock created from layers of deposited material that is cemented together
SERE	a successional sequence, including all the changes in plant communities, that follows a disturbance
SEROTINOUS CONES	cones that remain welded shut by a layer of resin and will open only when heated to a temperature above 120 degrees Fahrenheit

SOREDIA structures that function like spores and carry both fungal and algal cells for asexual reproduction in lichens

SPHEROIDAL WEATHERING a process by which coarse-grained igneous rocks become rounded by frequent periods of expansion and contraction in hot, dry climates

SQUAMULOSE LICHEN a lichen with a growth form intermediate between foliose and fruiticose lichens

STOLONS aboveground runners that give rise to new plants creating clones

SUBDUCTION the process by which denser oceanic crust is forced beneath less dense continental crust, eventually resulting in its melting deep below the Earth's surface

SUCCESSION a series of changes in plant communities that is initiated by some form of disturbance to an ecosystem

SUCCULENT a plant with fleshy leaves or stems that store large amounts of water

TARN a lake that fills a depression gouged into bedrock by a glacier

XERIC a term used to describe a dry environment

GEOLOGY

McPhee, John. *Rising from the Plains.* New York: Farrar, Straus, & Giroux, 1986.
A wonderful account of the geologic history of the Rocky Mountains in Wyoming and adjacent Montana.

_____. *Assembling California.* New York: Farrar, Straus, & Giroux, 1993.
A geologic history of California and the Sierra Nevada range.

Orr, Elizabeth and William Orr. *Geology of the Pacific Northwest.* New York: McGraw-Hill, 1996.
An authoritative description of the complex geology of this region.

Pielou, E. C. *After the Ice Age: The Return of Life to Glaciated North America.* Chicago: University of Chicago Press, 1991.
In-depth coverage of the deglaciation of North America.

Raymo, Chet, and Maureen Raymo. *Written in Stone: A Geological History of the Northeastern United States.* Old Saybrook: CT: The Globe Pequot Press, 1989.
A wonderful presentation of the tectonic history of the northeastern states.

GENERAL NATURAL HISTORY

Marchand, Peter. *North Woods: An Inside Look at the Nature of Forests in the Northeast.* Boston: Appalachian Mountain Club, 1987.
A great little book on the high-elevation ecosystems of the Northeast's mountains.

Whitney, Stephen. *A Sierra Club Naturalist's Guide: The Sierra Nevada.* San Francisco: Sierra Club Books, 1979.
A wealth of information on Sierra natural history.

_____. *A Sierra Club Naturalist's Guide: The Pacific Northwest.* San Francisco: Sierra Club Books, 1989.

Zwinger, Ann, and Beatrice Willard. *Land Above the Trees: A Guide to American Alpine Tundra.* Boulder, CO: Johnson Books, 1996.
A classic of natural history, and the inspiration behind The Granite Landscape.

FIELD GUIDES

Horin, Elizabeth and Kathleen Ort. *Sierra Nevada Wildflowers.* Missoula, MT: Mountain Press, 1998.
A fine field guide.

Kershaw, Linda et al. *Plants of the Rocky Mountains.* Edmonton, AB: Lone Pine, 1998.
A fine field guide to both flowering and nonflowering plants of the northern Rocky Mountains.

Larrison, Earl et al. *Washington Wildflowers.* Seattle: Seattle Audubon Society, 1974.
The taxonomy in this guide is dated, but it is still worth its weight in a backpack.

Slack, Nancy G., and Allison W. Bell. *AMC Field Guide to the New England Alpine Summits.* Boston: Appalachian Mountain Club, 1995.
Includes color photographs of most of the shrubs, flowers, lichens, and mosses described in this book.

Index

A

Abenaki tribes, 81

Abiotic environment, 52, 181

Absaroka Mountains, 129

Absaroka tribe, 129, 132

Abyssal plains, 100–101, 181

Acadia National Park, 12, 32, 48, 64, 76–90

    Beehive, 80, 84

    Black Woods Campground, 88, 89

    Bubble Pond, 89

    Bubble Rock, 80

    Eagle Lake, 82

    fire in, 82–85

    fogs, effect of, 85–89

    Great Head, 89

    Hunters Brook, 88

    Jordan Pond, 80

    origin of 4, 79–81

    Otter Cliffs, 82, 89

    Sand Beach, 80, 82

    wind, effect of, 82, 86, 89–90

Acadian Orogeny, 79, 80

Acidic substrates/soils, 14, 68–69

Adirondack Mountains (New York), 92, 93, 106–109

    jointing, 107

    old-growth forest, 108

    uplift of, 106–107

Adventitious buds, 71, 181

Agassiz, Louis, 42

Ahwahneechee tribe, 167–168

Algae, 54

Alpine glaciers, 38, 43–44, 46, 113

    Mount Chocorua, 99

    Wind River Range, 115–116

Alpine gooseberry, 164, 178

Alpine larch, 152–154, 177

Alpine phlox, 151, 175

Alpine pussytoes, 137, 175

Alpine reindeer lichen, 104, 175

American beech, 13, 47, 50, 87, 102, 179

American bistort, 120, 176

American mountain ash, 104, 178

Anatomy of Earth, 27–31

Andes Mountains, 30

Antarctic Ice Sheet, 42

Antarctica, 38, 43

Anthocyanin, 105, 181

Aphebian period, 174

Archipelagos, 101

Arctic Ocean, 43

Arctic willow, 139, 178

Arêtes, 116, 117, 118, 149, 181

Arizona, 66, 68

Ascomycetes, 54

Ash, 87–88. *See also* American mountain ash;
    White ash

Ashley, William, 130–131

Asia, 42–43

Aspen, 82, 84, 179

Avalonia, 79

B

Baja, Mexico, central desert of, 36

Baker, Mount (Washington), 145

Bald Knob (Montana), 134–135

Bald Peak (Maine), 77–78

Baneberry, red. *See* Red baneberry

Bar Harbor, Maine, 82

Basalt, 30, 181

Basin Lake, Montana, 135

Batholiths, 24, 30–31, 36, 93, 181

    Stuart, 146

    White Mountains, 101

    Wind River, 113, 114

Bear oak, 15, 16, 178

Bearberry, 59, 68, 161, 179

Bears, 16

Beartooth Mountains, 128–141

alpine bloom, 135–141

fires, effects of, 132–134

Beaufait, William, 69

Beaver, 130–131

Beech. *See* American beech

Beehive, Acadia National Park, 80, 84

Bell mountain heather, 146, 148, 178

Bidwell, John, 111–112

Big Sandy River and Lake, Wyoming, 112–113,
    116

Bilberry, bog. *See* Bog bilberry

Birch, 47, 82, 84, 87, 102. *See also* Black birch;
    Paper birch; Yellow birch

Black birch, 50, 178

Black chokeberry, 90, 178

Black crowberry, 178

    Acadia National Park, 86

    Adirondack Mountains, 93, 108–109

    White Mountains, 93, 102, 104–106

Black huckleberry, 15, 90, 178

Black Mountain (Vermont), 12–16

Black rock tripe, 146

Blake, William P., 167

Blueberry, 67, 68, 81. *See also* Dwarf blueberry;
    Low-bush blueberry

Bog bilberry, 93, 102, 104–106, 178

Boulder, Colorado, 66–67

Bridger, Jim, 126

Bridger Wilderness, 112

Bubble Pond, Acadia National Park, 89

Bubble Rock, Acadia National Park, 80

Bunchberry, 104, 176

C

Cadillac Mountain granite, 78

Cadillac Mountain (Maine), 76, 80, 85, 85, 88

Calcium, 13, 89

California, 66, 68. *See also* Yosemite National Park

California fuchsia, 162, 165, 176

Caloplaca, 139, 175

Cambrian period, 42, 174

Campion, moss. *See* Moss campion

Canada, 46

Canadian Shield, 101

Carboniferous period, 42, 174

Cascade Mountains, 73, 143, 145.
    See also Enchantment Lakes

Cashmere Crags (Washington), 143, 149,
    150

Cathedral Range (Washington), 166

Cedar. *See* Incense cedar; Northern white cedar;
    Western red cedar

Cenozoic era, 174

Champlain, Samuel de, 81

Champlain Mountain (Maine), 32, 82–83,
    84, 85

Chatter marks, 39–41, 80, 182

Chocorua, Mount, 11–12

Chokeberry. *See* Black chokeberry

Cinquefoil. *See* Shrubby cinquefoil;
    Snow cinquefoil; Three-toothed cinquefoil

Circular crevice communities, 60–62

Cirques, 99–100, 116, 182

Cladina, 87

Clear Lake, Wyoming, 110, 118

Clements, Frederic, 51–52

Climax, 51, 182

Colorado, 66–67

Colter, John, 130

Columbine, yellow. *See* Yellow columbine

Cone serotiny. *See* Serotinous cones

Coniferous trees and shrubs. *See also specific plants*
    layering, 119
    list of, 177–178

Connecticut River Valley, 14

Continental bedrock, 25

Continental crust, 28, 30. *See also* subduction

Continental Divide, 113, 122, 129

Continental drift, 25, 182

Continental glaciers, 38, 42–47, 115–116

Conway granite, 100

Core, Earth's, 28–29

Cranberry, mountain. *See* Mountain cranberry

Creeping juniper, 139, 177

Cretaceous period, 101, 174

Crevice communities, 60–62, 73–74
    Acadia National Park, 80, 85–86, 88–89
    Adirondack Mountains, 107
    Beartooth Mountains, 136–139
    Enchantment Lakes, 147–148
    White Mountains, 102–104
    Wind River Range, 121, 123–124
    Yosemite National Park, 164–165

Crevices, 78

Crowberry. *See* Black crowberry

Crust, Earth's. *See also* Continental crust;
    Oceanic crust
    plate tectonics, 23–27
    thickness of, 27

Crustose lichens, 54–62, 73, 74, 182
    Acadia National Park, 86
    Beartooth Mountains, 134
    White Mountains, 94–95, 98, 102
    Wind River Range, 121
    Yosemite National Park, 158

Cryptobiosis, 55–57, 73, 182

Cryptogamic carpets, 87, 88, 182

Crystal Creek, Washington, 151

Cyanobacteria, 54–55, 182

    White Mountains, 98, 102

    Wind River Range, 118

    Yosemite National Park, 158

D

De Monts, Sieur, 81

Deep Lake, Wyoming, 116, 118

Deer, 89

Depression communities, 17, 119–120

Devonian period, 174

Dickey Mountain (New Hampshire), 94

Disturbance, ecological, 50–52, 59, 65–66

Domes

    age of, 33, 81, 113–115, 166

    classic attributes of, 17

    in United States, map of, 6

Dorr Mountain (Maine), 84

Douglas fir, 144, 177

Drilling, deep-sea, 26–27

Dwarf blueberry, 139, 178

E

Eagle Lake, Acadia National Park, 82

Early blue violet, 120, 125, 176

Earth. *See also* Core, Earth's; Crust, Earth's; Mantle

    alignment with sun, 44–45

    anatomy of, 27–31

    magnetic field of, 26–27

Eastern hemlock, 50, 177

Eastern United States, 38, 46. *See also* New England;
    specific states

Eastern white pine, 13, 177

Ecological succession. *See* Succession

Elderberry, red. *See* Red elderberry

Elephant head, 120, 123, 140, 176

Elkhart Park, Wyoming, 122

Enchantment Lakes/Basin, 142–154

Engelmann spruce, 113, 119, 121, 132, 177

Environmental restoration project, 94–98

Epiphytes, 87–88, 182

Ericaceous, 132, 182

Eriogonum, Wright's. *See* Wright's eriogonum

Erosion

    of bedrock, 33, 34, 80

    due to hiking pressure, 108

    following fire, 132

    by glacier, 37

    Rocky Mountain formation and, 114

    stabilizing, 97

Europe, glacial coverage of, 42–43

Everglades, 66–68

Exfoliation, 34–36, 113, 164, 182

Expansion joints, 34–35, 60, 98, 183

Extrusive igneous rocks, 22

F

Farallon Plate, 146

Fathometers, 26, 100

Feldspar, 21–23, 30, 161

Fellfields, 121, 151, 183

Few-flowered shooting star, 140–141, 176

Fir. *See* Douglas fir; Red fir; Subalpine fir; White fir

Fires, granite exposed by, 52, 65–74

    Acadia National Park, 82–85

    Beartooth Mountains, 132–134

    Mount Chocorua, 99

    Seneca Lake, Wind River Range, 123

    Yosemite National Park, 162

Fireweed, 176

Firn, 73, 185

Fjords, 80

Florida Everglades, 66–68

Flowering trees and shrubs, 178–179.
     See also specific plants

Fog effect, Acadia National Park, 85–89

Foliose lichens, 54–55, 57–58, 62, 183
     Acadia National Park, 86, 89
     Beartooth Mountains, 139, 146
     Wind River Range, 121

Forest communities, 78, 87

Fortin, Dick, 95, 97

Fossils, 25

Foxtail pine, 157, 177

Fractals, 77, 183

Front Range (Colorado), 66–67

Fruiticose lichens, 55, 58, 62, 183
     Acadia National Park, 87
     Yosemite National Park, 161

Funaria, 73, 102, 145, 146, 162, 175

G

Galapagos Islands, 101

Giant sequoia, 66, 68, 177

Glacial boulders, 20, 80
     field of, 159–160, 164
     glaciers, embedded rocks/boulders in,
          39–41, 80

Glacial erratic, 42, 137, 183

Glacial grooves, 39, 78, 80, 183

Glacial notches, 41–42, 77–78, 80, 183

Glacial polish, 38–39, 49, 183
     Acadia National Park, 79, 80
     Bald Knob, Beartooth Mountains, 134
     Yosemite National Park, 158, 166

Glacial quarrying, 102, 116, 122, 146

Glacial stairways, 116–117,
     144

Glacial striations, 38, 39, 80, 166, 183

Glacial till, forests on, 87

Glaciated alpine valley, 117

Glaciation, 33–34, 37–43, 49, 115–116, 118
     fractal nature of landscape, 77–79
     Pleistocene (*See* Pleistocene glaciations)
     primary successional sites, creation of, 52

Glaciers
     alpine (*See* Alpine glaciers)
     continental, 38, 42–47, 115–116
     embedded rocks/boulders in, 39–41, 80
     erosion by, 37
     Lyell, 37, 42
     Snow Creek, 149–151

Gleason, Henry, 52

Global warming, 46

Globeflower, 140, 176

Gneiss, 132

Goats, mountain, 146–149

Golden Trout Camp, California, 157

Goldenrod, 123, 125, 176

Gooseberry, alpine. *See* Alpine gooseberry

Gorham Mountain (Maine), 84

Granite
     acid substrates/soil, 14, 68–69
     crystalline structure of, 21–23
     defined, 22
     exfoliation, 34–36, 113, 164
     expansion of, 34–35
     fires, exposed by (*See* Fires, granite exposed by)
     formation of, 23–24, 30
     origins of, 21–31, 79
     snow and ice, exposed by, 73

succession on (*See* Succession)

wind, exposed by, 74

Granite Peak (Montana), 134

Grasses, 58–59

Grasslands, 66, 68

Gravestones, 21–22

Great Head, Acadia National Park, 89

Great Meteor Seamount, 100–101

Green map lichen, 86, 121, 134, 175

Greenland, 38, 43

Greenleaf manzanita, 166, 178

Gulf Stream, 43

H

Hadrynian period, 174

Haircap moss, 16, 60, 61, 175

    White Mountains, 93, 94, 97, 104

    Yosemite National Park, 163

Hawaiian Islands, 30, 101

Haystack Mountain (Wyoming), 118

Heather. *See* Bell mountain heather; Pink mountain
    heather; Yellow mountain heather

Heaths, 17, 58–59, 68–69. *See also specific plants*

    Acadia National Park, 79, 90

    Adirondack Mountains, 108

    White Mountains, 93, 98, 102–106

Hebaceous flowering plants, 120, 175–177. *See also*
    specific plants

Helikian period, 113–114, 174

Hemlock, 47, 88, 108. *See also* Eastern hemlock;
    Mountain hemlock

Herb Robert, 13, 176

Herbs, 13, 58, 60. *See also specific plants*

Hess, Harry, 26, 27

Hetch Hetchy Valley, California, 168

Hickory, 67

Hiking pressure, effects of, 94–98, 107–109,
    147–148

Himalayas, 29, 43

Holly, mountain. *See* Mountain holly

Holocene epoch, 44, 174

Horn, 116, 117, 184

Hornblende, 22, 23, 161

Hot spots, 100–101, 115, 184

Huckleberry, 67, 68, 81. *See also* Black huckleberry;
    Mountain huckleberry

Hudson Bay, 101

Hunters Brook, Acadia National Park, 88

Hypsithermal, 46, 182

I

Ice, granite exposed by, 73

Ice ages, 42–47. *See also* Pleistocene glaciations

Ice creep, 73, 102, 120, 158, 184

Ice-blasting, 121, 146

Icicle Creek, Washington, 144

Igneous rock, 22–23, 29–30, 184

Incense cedar, 68, 177

India, 43

Indian paintbrush, 120, 176

Interglacial periods, 44–46, 49

Iron, 30

J

Jack pine, 66, 68–71, 84–85, 98–99, 177

Jackson Hole, Wyoming, 132

Jeffrey pine, 166, 177

John Muir Wilderness, 157

Joints, 41. *See also* Expansion joints

    Adirondack Mountains, 107

    Cascade Mountains, 146

    Wind River Range, 118, 125

Yosemite National Park, 159

Jordan Pond, Acadia National Park, 80

Juniper. *See* Creeping juniper; Western juniper

Jurassic period, 174

K

Kirtland's warblers, 66

L

Labrador tea, 93, 104, 178

Laramide Orogeny, 114–115

Larch, alpine. *See* Alpine larch

Laurel. *See* Mountain laurel; Sheep laurel

Laurentide Ice Sheet, 46, 79, 80, 88, 123

Lava, 22

Layering, 119, 184

Le Conte, Joseph, 167

Lecanora, 86, 121, 175

Leichtlin's mariposa lily, 162, 176

Lembert Dome, Yosemite National Park, 158–159

Leprechaun Lake, Washington, 145

Letharia, 166, 177

Lewis and Clark expedition, 130

Lichens, 48, 54–62. *See also* Crustose lichens;
  Foliose lichens; Fruiticose lichens; Squamulose
  lichens
  Acadia National Park, 85–88
  Adirondack Mountains, 108
  Beartooth Mountains, 134, 139, 146
  White Mountains, 93–95, 98, 102
  Wind River Range, 118, 121
  Yosemite National Park, 158, 161

Lily, Leichtlin's mariposa. *See* Leichtlin's mariposa
  lily

Limber pine, 121–122, 125, 138–139, 177

Little Annapurna Mountain (Washington), 142, 149

Lodgepole pine, 68–69, 71, 177
  Beartooth Mountains, 132
  Golden Trout Camp, 157
  Wind River Range, 112–113, 122–124
  Yosemite National Park, 168

Lomatium. *See* Martindale's lomatium

Low-bush blueberry, 15, 16, 58–59, 178
  Acadia National Park, 90
  White Mountains, 93–95, 102, 104

Lungwort, 87, 88, 175

Lyell Glacier, 37, 42

M

Magma, 23–24, 29–30, 184
  basalt, 30
  cooling of, 22–23
  magnetic alignment of minerals in, 26–27
  rhyolytic, 30, 186

Magnesium, 30

Magnetic field of Earth, 26–27

Maine. *See* Acadia National Park

Mantle, 28–29, 184

Mantle plumes, 28–29, 101

Manzanita, 68. *See also* Greenleaf manzanita;
  Pinemat manzanita

Maple, 47, 87–88, 102. *See also* Red maple;
  Striped maple; Sugar maple

Marigold, mountain marsh. *See* Mountain marsh
  marigold

Mariposa Battalion, 168

Martindale's lomatium, 151, 176

Mast years, 53, 184

McCellan, Mount, 149

Mertensia, 125, 176

Mesozoic era, 174

Mesquite, 66, 178

Metamorphic rock, 22, 82, 93, 184

Mica, 22, 23

Michigan, 64, 66

Microphylls, 146, 184

Mid-Atlantic Ridge, 27, 29, 185

Mid-oceanic ridges, 26–29
    cleft nature of, 26–27
    seafloor spreading at, 26–28

Midwestern United States, 46

Miwok tribe, 167–168

Montana. *See* Beartooth Mountains

Moraines, recessional, 151

Moss campion, 121, 178

Mosses, 62, 73. *See also specific plants*
    Acadia National Park, 85, 87
    dry-sited, 60
    pincushion, 58, 60
    White Mountains, 94–95, 98

Mount Chocorua (New Hampshire), 98–100

Mount Desert Island, Maine, 12, 76–90
    fogs, effect of, 85–89
    origin of, 79–81
    wind, effect of, 82, 86, 89–90

Mount Welch (New Hampshire), 94–98

Mountain cranberry, 86, 93, 102–104, 178

Mountain goats, 146–148

Mountain hemlock, 164, 177

Mountain holly, 104, 179

Mountain huckleberry, 132, 179

Mountain laurel, 13–15, 179

Mountain Man, Museum of the, 130

Mountain marsh marigold, 136, 140, 176

Mountain men, 129–132

Mountain pennyroyal, 162, 176

Mountains, formation of. *See* Orogeny

Muir, John, 122, 157, 167–169

Mullein, 56–57, 176

Mutualism, 54, 185

N

Naiad Lake, Washington, 144

Narrowleaf stonecrop, 146, 165, 176

Native Americans, fire use by, 67

New England, 46, 47, 56, 67, 88. *See also* Acadia
    National Park; Adirondack Mountains; White
    Mountains

New England Seamounts, 101

New Hampshire. *See* White Mountains

Nightmare Needles (Washington), 151

Nonflowering plants, 175. *See also specific plants*

Noonmark Mountain (New York), 92, 107–109

North America, glacial coverage of, 42–43

North American Plate, 101, 146, 166

North Baldface Mountain (New Hampshire),
    104, 106

Northern Hemisphere, 43, 45–46

Northern white cedar, 78, 88–89, 177

Norumbega Mountain (Maine), 77

Nunataks, 119, 122, 185

O

Oak, 59, 67. *See also* Bear oak; Red oak;
    White oak

Oceanic crust. *See also* Subduction
    basaltic nature of, 30
    magnetic alignment of minerals in, 26–27
    rifting zones, 26

Off-trail hiking, rules for, 97

Old-growth forest, 108

Ordovician period, 42, 174

Oregon Trail, 111

Orogeny, 29–31, 33, 79–81, 100–101, 113–116, 167, 185

Ostriches, African, 25

Otter Cliffs, Acadia National Park, 82, 89

Outcrop communities, 54–62, 78

    Acadia National Park, 78

    Adirondack Mountains, 109

    White Mountains, 94–98, 102–106

Ouzel Lake, Montana, 134, 135

P

Pacific Plate, 33, 166

Paintbrush. *See* Indian paintbrush; Rosy paintbrush

Paleozoic era, 174

Panama, Isthmus of, 43

Pangaea, 25, 166

Paper birch, 84, 98, 179

Parkman Mountain (Maine), 78

Pemetic Mountain (Maine), 89, 90

Pennyroyal, mountain. *See* Mountain pennyroyal

Penobscot Bay, Maine, 78, 87

Permian period, 174

Phenocrysts, 161, 185

Pigwackets tribe, 100

Pikas, 139–140

Pincushion plants, 58, 60

Pine, 17, 47, 59, 68–70, 82. *See also* Eastern white pine; Foxtail pine; Jack pine; Jeffrey pine; Limber pine; Lodgepole pine; Pitch pine; Ponderosa pine; Red pine; Western white pine; Whitebark pine

    forest, succession in, 50, 53

    stump-sprouting, 84

Pine bark beetle, 66

Pinedale, Wyoming, 125, 130

Pinemat manzanita, 163, 164, 179

Pink monkey flower, 151, 176

Pink mountain heather, 120, 123, 140, 146, 149, 179

Pitch pine, 15, 64, 68–69, 71–72, 82–85, 88–90, 177

Plant communities, 68. *See also* Crevice communities; Outcrop communities; Succession

    depression, 17, 119–120

    forest, 78, 87

    pincushion, 58, 60

Plant Succession: An Analysis of the Development of Vegetation (Clements), 51–52

Plants, list of, 175–179. *See also* specific plants

Plate tectonics, 23–27, 29, 43, 47, 113–115, 146, 185

Pleistocene epoch, 174

Pleistocene glaciations, 42–47, 80, 123, 167

Polly Dome, Yosemite National Park, 159–164

Polytrichum, 87

Ponderosa pine, 66–67, 166, 177

Potholes, White Mountains, 98

Precambrian era, 113–114, 174

Primary succession, 52–54, 59, 185

Prusik Peak (Washington), 147

Pussypaws, 161, 164, 176

Q

Quartz, 21–22, 23, 30

Quartzite, 22

Quaternary period, 174

R

Raisin. *See* Wild raisin

Raymo, Chet and Maureen, 25

Reading the Forested Landscape (Wessels), 18

Red baneberry, 13, 176

Red elderberry, 166, 179

Red fir, 161, 177

Red maple, 84, 88, 98, 179

Red oak, 15, 98, 179

Red pine, 15, 177

Red spruce, 78, 87–90, 94, 98, 177

Reindeer lichen, 16, 58, 60, 61, 93, 94, 98, 175.
    See also Alpine reindeer lichen

Relay floristics, 51–52, 54, 185

Rheas, South American, 25

Rhizinae, 55, 185

Rhizomes, 69, 186

Rhodora, 104, 179

Rhyolytic magma, 30, 186

Rifting zones, 23, 26, 28, 29, 186

Roche moutonnée, 40, 41, 80, 186

Rock, types of, 22–24.
    See also Granite

Rock tripe, 86, 175

Rocky Mountains, 66–67, 113–116, 157

Roseroot, 137, 176

Rosy paintbrush, 140, 151, 176

Round Mountain (New York), 107–108

Royal Arches, Yosemite Valley, 34–36

Rune Lake, Washington, 151

Rushes, 146

Russel, Israel, 149

Russell, Osborne, 129–130

Russell Creek, 129, 132

S

Saco River, 100

St. Croix River, 81

St. Helens, Mount, 30

Sand Beach, Acadia National Park,
    80, 82

Sandwich Range Conservation Association (SRCA),
    94

Saxifrage. *See* Spotted saxifrage; Tolmie's saxifrage

Schists, 12, 13

Scrimshaw, Nat, 94, 95

Sea level, changes in, 46

Seafloor spreading, 26–28, 186

Seafloors, mapping of, 25–26

Seamounts, 26, 101, 186
    Great Meteor Seamount, 100–101
    New England, 101

Secondary succession, 52–54, 186

Sedges, 146, 164

Sedimentary rock, 22, 186

Seismic activity, Adirondack Mountains, 106–107

Selaginella, 164, 175

Senaca Lake, Wyoming, 122–126

Sequoia. *See* Giant sequoia

Sere, 50–62, 186

Serotinous cones, 69–71, 84, 98, 186

Shad, 98, 179

Sheep, 168

Sheep laurel, 90, 104, 179

Shoshone tribe, 129, 132

Shrubby cinquefoil, 123, 179

Shrubs. *See* Trees and shrubs

Sierra Nevada, 30, 33, 115, 157, 166–168. *See also*
    Yosemite National Park

Silicates, 30

Silurian period, 174

Slate, 21, 22

Snow, granite exposed by, 73

Snow cinquefoil, 139–140, 176

Snow Creek, Washington, 142

Snow Creek Glacier (Washington), 149–151

Snowfields, effects on plant life of, 134–136, 139–140, 145–146, 151, 161

Sohm Abyssal Plain, 101

Soil, formation of, 57–58

Somes Sound (Maine), 79, 80

Somesville granite, 79

Sonar, 25–26

Soredia, 57, 187

South America, 43

South Baldface Mountain (New Hampshire), 101–106

South Bubble Mountain (Maine), 80

South Pass, Wyoming, 111–112

Southeastern United States, 17

Southwest Harbor Granite, 79

Southwestern United States, 17, 66, 68

Sphagnum, 87, 175

Spheroidal weathering, 36–37, 187

Spotted saxifrage, 137, 176

Spruce, 59. *See also* Engelmann spruce; Red spruce

Squamulose lichens, 55, 58, 60, 187

Stark, Bill and Peg, 149

Steeple Peak (Wyoming), 110, 118

Stolons, 137, 187

Stone Mountain, Georgia, 17

Stone walls, 13

Stonecrop, narrowleaf. *See* Narrowleaf stonecrop

Striped maple, 78, 179

Stuart, Mount, 144

Stuart batholith, 146

Stuart Range, 143–144

Subalpine fir, 132, 145, 178

Subduction, 23–24, 26, 29–30, 33, 187
    of Avalonia, 79
    Cascade Mountains, 146

low-angle, 113–114
    Rocky Mountain formation and, 113–115
    Yosemite, 166

Succession, 187
    primary and secondary, 52–54, 59
    theories of, 49–52

Succulent, 137, 187

Sugar maple, 13, 50, 94, 108, 179

Surficial crevices, 34

Surficial sections
    exfoliation of, 34–36
    thickness of, 34

T

Talisman Lake, Washington, 151–152

Talus, 139–140, 164

Target lichen, 86–87, 175

Tarns, 116, 118, 135, 144, 187

Temple Pass, Wyoming, 121

Temple Peak (Wyoming), 110, 119

Tenaya Lake, California, 156, 159, 164

Tertiary period, 174

Thompson, Rich, 129, 132, 134–135

Thoreau, Henry David, 49–50

Three-toothed cinquefoil, 85, 86, 104, 106, 176

Thunderstorms, 119–122, 125–126, 151

Tioga Pass, Yosemite National Park, 158

Tolmie's saxifrage, 146, 177

Trees and shrubs. *See also specific plants*
    acid-tolerant, 59
    coniferous (*See* Coniferous trees and shrubs)
    dry-sited, 59, 60, 62, 139
    flowering, 178–179
    hardy shrubs, 58–59
    spiraling of, 123–124, 132

Triassic period, 174

Trout, 135

Tuolomne Meadows, Yosemite National Park, 158, 168

Tuolomne River, Grand Canyon of, 33, 159, 165–166

Twin Lake, Montana, 135

U

Uniform ecology of domes, 12

Upper Snow Lake, Washington, 146

V

Vermont, 12–16

Violet, early blue. *See* Early blue violet

Viviane Lake, Washington, 144, 147

Volcanic activity, 22, 24, 29–30

    hot spots, 100–101, 115, 184

    primary successional sites, creation of, 52

W

Wallflower, 120, 177

Walter, David, 34–36

Washburn Point, Yosemite Valley, 34–36

Waterville Valley, New Hampshire, 94

Weed, C. L., 168

Wegener, Alfred, 24–25, 27

Western juniper, 164–166, 178

Western red cedar, 144, 178

Western spring beauty, 136–137, 140, 177

Western United States, 38, 129–132. *See also specific states*

Western white pine, 159–161, 178

Whalebacks, Acadia National Park, 80

White ash, 88, 89

White cedar, 90

White fir, 66, 178

White Mountain National Forest, 94, 97

White Mountains (New Hampshire), 93, 94–106

    Mount Welch, 94–98

    origin of, 100–101

    South Baldface Mountain, 101–106

White oak, 15, 179

White pine, 15, 50, 78, 82, 87, 88, 98

Whitebark pine, 145, 152, 158, 178

Whitney, Josiah Dwight, 167

Wild raisin, 104, 179

Wind

    Acadia National Park, 82, 86, 89–90

    granite exposed by, 74

    Wind River Range, 121

Wind River Range, 74, 110–126, 129

    Big Sandy River and Lake, Wyoming, 112–113, 116

    Bridger Wilderness, 112

    Clear Lake, 110, 118

    Deep Lake, 116, 118

    formation of, 113–116

    Seneca Lake, 122–126

Wisconsin Glaciation, 46

Wounded Knee, 112

Wright's eriogonum, 164, 177

Written in Stone (Raymo), 25

Wyoming. *See* Wind River Range

X

Xeric, 187

Y

Yarrow, 123, 125, 177

Yellow birch, 78, 88, 179

Yellow columbine, 139–140, 176

Yellow mountain heather, 140, 179

Yellow pine. *See* Jack pine; Lodgepole pine;
    Pitch pine
Yellowstone National Park, 115, 129, 132–134
Yosemite National Park, 20, 33–38, 73, 156–170
    fires, 162
    history of, 166–170
    Lembert Dome, 158–159

Polly Dome, 159–164
Tenaya Lake, 159
Tioga Pass, 158
Tuolomne Meadows, 158, 168
Tuolomne River, Grand Canyon of, 33, 159
Yosemite Valley, 34–36, 167–168

About the Author and Illustrator

Tom Wessels is a professor of ecology in the Department of Environmental Studies at Antioch New England Graduate School, and has conducted workshops in landscape ecology throughout the United States for more than twenty-five years. He is chair of the Robert and Patricia Switzer Foundation, which fosters environmental leadership through graduate fellowships and grants. He is also the author of *Reading the Forested Landscape: A Natural History of New England.*

Brian D. Cohen is a printmaker, teacher, director of Two Rivers Printmaking Studio, and publisher of the Bridge Press in Westminster Station, Vermont. His etchings and limited edition letterpress books are in major university, museum, and private collections. Brian's etchings and drawings also appear in *Reading the Forested Landscape.*

A Note on the Type

The text for this book was composed in Minion, designed by Robert Slimbach. The display type was set in The Sans, designed by Lucas de Groot and published by FontShop International.

Brian D. Cohen's drawings were made on clay-coated board with ink wash and black pencil. The clay coating allowed him to cut through the surface to achieve very fine details and highlights.